BEAUTIFULLY BROKEN

OVERCOMING ABUSE & STEPPING INTO THE LIGHT

KELLY FRANKLIN

Print ISBN: 979-8-9912197-4-7

Works Cited:

(Ecclesiastes 7:3, The Scriptures. Institute for Scripture Research. 2016)

(Exodus 3:7-8, The Catholic Study Bible. Third Edition)

(Psalm 4:8, The Catholic Study Bible, Third Edition.)

(Isaiah 43:18-21, The Catholic Study Bible. Third Edition)

(Psalms 4:8, The Scriptures Bible).

("Love Bombing." Dictionary.cambridge.org, Dictionary, Cambridge, https://dictionary.cambridge.org/us/dictionary/english/love-bombing.Accessed 16 Mar. 2024.)

("Heal." Merriam-Webster.com Dictionary, Merriam-Webster, https://www.merriam-webster.com/dictionary/heal. Accessed 16 Mar. 2024.)

CONTENTS

THE BEGINNING

THE TRIALS

BIG CHANGES

PHOENIX RISING

THE BEAUTIFUL

APPENDIX

This book is dedicated to my mom Sharon, sister Ann, and best friend Tami. Thank you for always being there for me, especially in the early mornings and late nights. Thank you for being the women who provided a firm foundation when I felt most alone.

THE BEGINNING

DISCLAIMER FOR BEAUTIFULLY BROKEN

This book has been written from my perspective and the events of
how I remembered them.
All names, dates, timelines, and amounts have been changed to
protect the identities of those within this book.

INTRODUCTION

I love what I do! Sitting here with you is the pinnacle of my day. There isn't a moment that has gone by that I haven't had you on my mind. You are the reason this book exists. You are an extraordinary person who has been through hell and back. You are a champion, and no matter what kind of trauma you're fighting to get out of, know it can be done and overcome.

The person you are right now is not the person you are meant to be. You don't have to stay in the place you are and feel as though your home is a frigid, dark prison cell of abuse. You might be wondering how you ended up here or what you did to deserve what you're going through. This is the truth: no one deserves to be abused, ever. You did nothing to deserve the hell you're suffering currently.

Abuse is a monster slowly creeping into your life. It studies your every move, and when you least expect it, BAM, it pounces on you. It devours your life and everything around you to where you lose your zest for life. Food loses its taste, sleep escapes you, breathing hurts, your work is pushed off for another day, and you merely exist because the pain is excruciating. The pain is horrendous – physically and emotionally – and you wonder if you'll ever make it out alive.

Some days you might be begging God to take your life, but He's not done with you yet.

If you're sitting here with me right now, God has a purpose for you. There is an anointing on your life, and God has you right where He wants you. He wants this book in your hands. I know because when I was searching for answers, I didn't find any and needed a book like this. He wants me here with you. Thank you for picking up this book so I can walk this journey with you.

Trauma is hell on earth. There is nothing like slowly losing your mind, soul, health, and ability to function while crying out to God, begging Him to fix the plummeting roller coaster you are currently riding.

You stood in line for the roller coaster on a warm, sunny day as the sun kissed your cheeks. Looking up with your eyes closed, you basked in the glory of the moment. You thought you had finally found the one person who would love you forever. Then quickly, you open your eyes wider as the line starts moving forward. You thought this was the moment you had been waiting for as you raced up the brown, wooden stairs, taking monumental strides to reach the final platform as if you were racing to the finish line. *I must be first* is what you were thinking. You pause for a moment, and then you quickly usher yourself to the first car in your relationship.

As the bars on the wooden roller coaster rise, the metal gates open. Your heart is racing! It's beating so fast you question whether you should step inside the car. You pause for a second and then step into the car. Your heart is pounding; the breaths you take are shallow as you take your seat. You secure your purse next to your waist and buckle the thick, orange seat belt. The old, cushy lap bar is lowered and permanently locked. Now you can't get out! You're stuck on this ride until something astronomical occurs. Your chest tightens, throat thickens, and panic enters your life forever. You gotta get off this ride! Please HELP! *Why won't someone help me?* you think.

This is what it's like being in any relationship defined by abuse. You can't get out until one or both of you says to hell with it or worse. No matter what, you MUST get out of this relationship.

Wherever you are at this point, know that I've been there. The light at the end of the tunnel is within reach, so you must keep going. You must do everything in your power to get free from the abuse.

It can be scary, and you don't know what or where you will end up, but the place you are sitting is not it. Take my hand, and I'll go with you, matching you step for step. Let's do this together.

My hope for this book is to hold your hand as we escape abuse together. I want you to know you are not alone, my friend. I have wasted away in what feels like the darkest, coldest dungeon sunk into the depths of the ocean, unable to breathe. This is the place where you are. You are suffering through life, not living but surviving. You are a shell of who you once were, so let's get you out of this sorrow and into living a life you have only dreamt of.

You don't have to be ready or have everything in order. The courage is within you. It's time to be strong and courageous. It's time for you to get your FREEDOM BACK! It's time to get your LIFE back! Are you ready? Are you with me? Let's do this! Everything you want is on the other side of fear. Feel the fear, and do it anyway, JUMP!

1

PREP FOR THE JOURNEY

Before you read my story, I must confess that it's been one of the hardest things I've ever done. Finding the time to write my story is hard enough while writing it is even more challenging, but neither of those is why it was difficult for me to write this book. I've wrestled with exactly what to put in and what to leave out, in terms of details. I have children, family, great friends, and I go to a great church. I did not want to write a tell-all book that would expose me as not the perfect person they might think I am.

However, when I stopped thinking of myself and put my focus on you, dear reader, without knowing it, you encouraged me to write my story, warts and all. So, at the risk of being embarrassed, you are holding the truest account of my life in your hands, sourced directly from journals that captured key moments and the emotions of the time. Although it has been painful and I've been embarrassed, I have decided to let everything out—the good, the bad, the ugly, and even the private ugly things I thought I'd never tell a soul.

I risk showing you this because my focus is to motivate you. I have been blessed to have found inspiration from others, and now I'm attempting to bring some to you. I believe you can provoke a blessing and that you have it in you, the vision, to live the life your Creator designed especially for you. Contained in this book is not only my story, but motivation and inspiration you can draw from to live a better life.

2

THE JOURNEY

I couldn't believe it! It had been four months since my college engagement ended. Dean, my former fiancé who lived with me, would strut into the apartment acting as if there was nothing wrong. I tried desperately to connect with him, but nothing worked. He was like an empty vessel sitting on a shelf. Dean's eyes were open, but nobody was home. I sat in our small one-bedroom apartment with the sunlight streaming through our sliding glass doors, thinking of something to say. But NOTHING came to mind except cold, empty sensations.

I was glad when he left. I came home from teaching children to find Dean loading all of his belongings into his crew cab truck. He said he was being deployed, since he was in the military, but I knew better. He had submitted his paperwork to return to the war zone he referred to as "home." Instead of fighting Dean on staying, I sat my things down and helped him pack. If he didn't want to remain in the home we had built together, then I would expedite the process of getting him to his future a little more quickly.

Don't get me wrong; I loved this man but if he was adamant to pack while I was at work, never mentioning a word to me that he would be leaving soon, then there was no reason for me to fight a losing battle. I never felt a emotional connection to Dean while he was home so he might as well be on his way. Unfortunately, I feel like the only reason he entered our relationship was so he had someone missing him while he was on deployment when we got together.

I was in college when we got together. At first, it was wonderful. He spent time arranging romantic dates, but once he returned from deployment, he had changed. I thought things would change once we moved in together, but they got worse. He became distant and went to the bar with his friends. So, yes, I'd rather be single and alone than sit next to someone who was supposed to love me and wouldn't.

He didn't try to love me or show up when I needed him. Maybe it was the chaos of war that made him feel comfortable or in control, but I knew I couldn't put my life on hold waiting for someone to love me when it was never going to happen. Setting Dean free and moving forward was my heart's anthem. He left, and I never looked back. I don't miss the nights he would catapult himself off the bed screaming, "GET DOWN," as he waved his arms around wielding an imaginary gun. I mentioned that he should get checked for PTSD, but he never did. Either way, those days are gone, and I'm thankful.

Fast Forward

I had a new zest for life after my fiancé left. Going out and spending time with my family was the medicine I needed to get my groove back. Dean was gone, and our should-have-been-wedding date coming and going, it was no skin off my back. I was sad at first but eventually saw this as a blessing in disguise. It was better to have loved and lost than be stuck in an unthinkable marriage. He even took my engagement ring with him, so I really hoped the next woman he met enjoyed it. As embarrassing as it is to admit, he never got the ring sized to fit me. He told me he didn't have time to do it then why propose to me? He was a real winner, and I knew how to pick them. I might as well have slapped a target on my back that read "Will foster any man-child until he finds his forever home somewhere else." I'm joking but it's true.

20

I say this because in the midst of this amazing new life I had been creating, another helpless soul discovered me. Some days I wish I wasn't a kind person with a big heart. You see, it was my heart that landed me in this putrid-smelling mess that wreaked of days-old vomit to begin with.

The Hospital

I was 24 and had always tried to help those in need, as I was taught as a kid. I'm the person that goes above and beyond until it's a detriment to myself. A little side note: Choosing others over yourself to a fault is not something to be praised for. It's a cry for help, so be the person you wished you had in your life to help you and not the other way around.

Back to my thought, I would go above and beyond to help others. This is how, after Dean, I met the man who I feel was sent by Satan himself to destroy me. Every fiber of my being was destroyed, and I had to fight like hell to get the woman back that I used to know, except this version was extremely improved from the younger woman I knew before.

The woman I am now would be the one who would hug the younger one. The younger version of me was doing the best she could, unknowingly loving a skilled, manipulative liar who used his kids to get ahead in life. Pathetic excuse for a man. Who uses their kids to get ahead in life? I know who, a loser! Yup, a big fat loser who was only worried about his image and not the young toddlers in his care. The version of me now would sit and listen as her heart broke. The only thing that means the world to her is her family, and she could have had that without going through the pain she experienced. She wanted to be loved and didn't want to end up with a "psychology" degree at the end of her marriage.

I landed in this situation because I was helping a co-worker, Trish, move out of her house after her son suffered a devastating injury. He had sustained head trauma and had been rushed to the children's hospital in downtown Indianapolis, Indiana; her son was a toddler at the time. I received a phone call one late April night. I heard panic in her voice as she said, "Kelly, can you come to the hospital? I've called everyone, and I can't get a hold of anyone." She needed me so I immediately grabbed my keys and purse and headed out the door. My yummy strawberry wine cooler would have to wait, as my friend needed me.

I jumped in my old 92' Buick, slammed the door, and raced off to the hospital. I didn't know what to expect when I got there, but I had a feeling in the pit of my stomach it wasn't going to be good. When I arrived, I remember feeling nervous, sick to my stomach, and wishing I had drunk that wine cooler to calm my nerves. I wanted to be anywhere but there in the hospital.

I saw my friend, Trish, sitting on the couch as I rushed over and asked her, "What happened?" She told me that the police had called her while she was at work to inform her there had been an accident involving her son. Something happened at home while the babysitter was watching him. They let her know they were rushing him to the hospital because his brain was swelling. Once she got to the hospital, she had to wait for her baby boy to come out of emergency surgery.

We waited for what seemed like hours for his surgery to be finished. When the doctor came out, she was a real treat. No seriously, she was a royal you-know-what with a capital B. Instead of coming out to let us know how my friend's son ended up in this position, she started accusing us of physically harming this little boy. The doctor said, "I don't know who did this, but it was one of you!" I usually like being around doctors because for the most part they are very helpful, but this one had some screws loose. She was way off base accusing either of us of hurting a child.

I told the doctor I had not had contact with this child for six months and her accusation was ridiculous. I was simply here out of courtesy for a friend who needed my help. I had slept all night in the emergency room, waiting for this little guy to be alright, and I felt resentful. My friend knew I hadn't done anything wrong either.

I couldn't believe this doctor. She could be angry, upset, or any other emotion, but she wasn't going to accuse me of shaking a baby back and forth, snapping his head back so hard it caused swelling. This wasn't going to happen. I back-talked the doctor and put her in her place in terms of if I did anything to this little boy. The doctor had to cut a piece of Caleb's skull off of his body and keep him under close observation, but this didn't mean she could treat me, or anyone, as though I was trash on the street with false accusations. I stayed for a few more hours, then left because I had to go to work.

When I walked out of the hospital into the barely lit parking garage, I couldn't believe everything that transpired. I didn't want to nor did I go back to the hospital again, and I never did. I never again went back to help my friend because of a doctor who would rather accuse people instead of helping their patient's family. Hard job or not, this is not how you get people to work with you.

The Hail Mary Pass

Once my friend got her bearings together, she called and asked if I would help her move out of the house she had been sharing with her boyfriend. Being the person I am, I helped her. I also had recently moved into a two-bedroom apartment so I was going to allow her and the baby to use the available space I had until she could find a place of her own. This is how I met JJ, the man who was sent into my life by Satan himself to destroy everything I was.

He was another one of her helpful friends that wanted to see her safe and out of the situation she was living in. JJ seemed like a stand-up guy who wanted the best for everyone. I will say that since I had just broken up with my fiancé at the time, it was nice being around a man who wanted to help. There was no way I could know he would turn my life into a living hell.

JJ was always scripting his life. His perceptions about himself were one hundred percent correct in his eyes because he chose not to see the harm he was doing to others. He knew what he was doing, but he didn't care. He would tell me I mattered but then he would ignore me and go out with his friends or chat with others on his phone. He would also "breadcrumb" me on Saturdays. He would ignore me all week then magically want to spend time with me hiking and buying me dinner but when Sunday rolled around, he acted as though I didn't exist, again. He wouldn't return my text messages, and he repeated this cycle weekly.

On the flip side, when he wanted a new vehicle, he would be extra attentive. He would take me out to dinner then take me to the dealership to sign the purchase agreement papers. He even took me to Camping World on Mara's graduation day because she didn't give him a ticket. He wasn't included and tried to fill that void by trying to force me into buying a Teardrop Camper. I refused to buy the camper and I could feel his loathing for me.

Everyone he knows he uses to serve him, and that was it. He used his "good deeds" to help others or so I thought. He wasn't actually helping but was gathering attention from others also known as supply because he deeply cared what others thought of him. He wanted and needed their validation. He was a shell of a human being that was only filled up with the opinions of what other people thought of him. Helping others was his Hail Mary pass.

Sam didn't appreciate my blunt delivery, but I didn't give a rip. I was over his cocky attitude bossing the women around. I didn't want some chicken-legged armed man standing in a truck, telling me what to do as I carried everything out and he stood in the bed of the truck. Nice guy! What man stands in the back of a truck barking orders at women. Oh, right, a guy with short man syndrome. Honestly, my friend and I could have handled this on our own, but these tools decided they would come along to help.

That was how he met me. He showed up with his friend Sam. Ugh! At the time, Sam was seriously into me, and I was not feeling it; this also created a bit of competition between JJ and Sam. I bluntly told Sam I wasn't in the mood to be bossed around by another opinionated man who didn't have a backbone.

As I helped my friend move out of her house, Sam stood in the back of the truck pointing to where I should place each item. His screechy little voice got on my nerves. He demanded I put one thing here and another there but refused to get out of the truck while the women were doing all the lifting. He showed up to "help" someone in a tough situation but he refused to enter the house. I'm over men who tell women what to do but won't put any sweat in. Just showing up doesn't get the job done. Also, setting off his taser next to my eye didn't help either. It made me feel like I had to fight to protect myself.

I was glad when we reached the end of the day, as I was ready to return the truck and turn in for the night. I never wanted to move anyone again.

Date Night

After my friend Trish got everything settled in my apartment, she invited the guys back over to thank them. I didn't mind if they came this time because they were coming over to enjoy a meal and not boss me around. I made pizza burgers with my mom's yummy recipe. This was one of my favorite things I ate when growing up, so what better way to show appreciation than share it with people who helped my friend move, even if I wasn't a fan of one of them at the time.

We spent the night talking and getting to know each other, which went pretty well for the most part. After a while, the guys were done and took off for the night, and we girls stayed up talking.

We talked about the guys' personalities and who we thought went well with whom. Trish and I clearly liked the same guy, and she was pushing the skinny, chicken-legged one on me. I wasn't having it, but at the time, she said she wouldn't go out with the other guy until I went on a date with the skinny one. Ick!

Twos a Crowd

Unfortunately, I went out on a date with the super skinny guy I could break in half with my elbow, even though I wasn't attracted to him at all. I wanted to hurry up and get this pity date over with. I know it sounds bad, but I thought I was helping my friend again. However, it turned out I was punishing myself and didn't want to be there in the first place.

After this clown Sam picked me up, I wasn't with him for more than thirty minutes, and he was already talking to me about attending Christmas with his family. YIKES! He was also talking about having kids with me. Oh my gosh, I wanted to jump out of the car and run down the street, getting as far away from him as I could. I hope I'm not the only one that has been on a date like that.

After our date was over, I don't recall ever talking to him again, date-wise. I didn't see myself with him, and he definitely wasn't my type. This was the first and last time I ever went on a pity date. It's not my thing, and I won't be doing it again. Bullet dodged!

The Phone Call

Fast forward, a few weeks went by, and my friend Trish did not want to go on the date with the other guy, JJ, who had come to my apartment. I was ticked because she wouldn't go out with him after I went out on a date with his friend Sam. JJ ended up asking her for my phone number but she wouldn't give it to him. He was determined to get my phone number, so he called Sam, the guy I went with on the pity date.

Sam was a pain in my backside and gave JJ my number. Thanks, Sam, not!

This is where our story starts to change. JJ and I spent weeks talking on the phone, and he came over to my apartment for short visits. He seemed like a wonderful guy and helped his sister Barb when she called because she had a flat tire in Bloomington, Indiana. He said, "I gotta go help my sister, or I'm going to get my butt kicked by my dad." We ended our night and he took off.

Dating

Three weeks later, we started officially dating. I thought I had found my Prince Charming. Our first date was to his cousin's graduation party at a park in Monroe County, Indiana. I met a lot of his family that day and loved his cute great-uncle, George. I would have rather gone off with him looking back. At least he knew how to appropriately introduce himself to a lady and be a gentleman.

This party seemed to solidify us as a couple, as we got the family's approval. Life went fast after this. Probably too fast to where I didn't realize I was caught up in a tornado of lies. A tornado that would be used to destroy my life. I was sucked into the chaos and couldn't see a way out.

THE TRIALS

3

TANKED

Three years after our marriage, JJ would be passed out drunk every day I left for work. I could smell the stench of whiskey seeping out of his pores. The disgusting stench left sweat stains on his pillow, as his body worked overtime to expel the poison from his body. Although he did this so many times, his boss still had to use his emergency contact to come to our house and find his drunken body still passed out in bed. He should have been to work at 8:00 a.m., and there he lay at 10:30 a.m., too intoxicated to get up and go to work. JJ was out of control, and no one could stop him. Everyone was powerless to get him to stop drinking once his dad had died.

Eventually, he was fired from his job. This sucked for me because not only did I have to support us both, but he also had more time to drink since he wasn't working. There were plenty times he wouldn't message me back and I would worry that I'd go home to find him dead.

Sure enough, once free from his day job, he was drunk 96% of the time. I left for work, and he was drunk in bed, then when I arrived home from work, he was wasted in the ugly, brown lounge chair he sat in. He had drool running down his face most of the time, and I'd wipe it off with a blanket and then cover him up. When I saw him in this condition, it repulsed me. I couldn't believe the man I had fallen in love with, who had so much zest for life, was reduced to a drunken fool sitting in a chair, pretending like he had it made. He wanted the work-from-home life, a choice that was sucking the life out of him. He had zero drive and no respect for himself, God, his wife, or his children whom he had with an ex-girlfriend and an ex-wife. He became the one person I hated most. I took my wedding vows seriously, so I stuck by him for better or for worse and now I ask myself, "What did these vows cost me?"

These vows cost me a lot of lessons I wished that I didn't have to learn. Some days I wished I could go back in time and rewrite history. The days I pulled myself out of bed, watching him sleep off his drunken stupor from the night before, pained me. I dreaded driving away from our little yellow house on Melody Street because I never knew if it would be the last time I would see him. I was always scared to come home and walk through the door thinking he was dead from alcohol poisoning or a gunshot to the head. The second-to-last time he ended up in the emergency room, the doctor told him if he didn't stop drinking, he was likely to develop pancreatitis and his body would start shutting down. Unfortunately, he didn't stop drinking.

The doctor gave him some pain meds, which helped for a little while until they wore off. Honestly, I preferred him on the pain meds because he was a kinder person and at least I got to laugh with him. At times, his behavior was dangerous while on the pain meds but for the moment, my life didn't suck so much. Try driving a guy doped up on meds from the hospital to home with a fifty-minute drive, trying to keep his hands off my gear shift. That was a fun ride home as he grabbed the shifter and forced my car to slow down on the interstate. YIKES!

JJ's sobriety didn't last long, if ever. I found my then-husband waking me up at 2:00 a.m., begging me to take him to the hospital. He was grabbing his chest and telling me there was something wrong. I hurried up and got him to the nearest fire station, and they loaded him into the ambulance and raced him to the emergency room.

While I sat waiting for the doctors to run tests and administer more pain meds, this emergency doctor also told him to stop drinking but he wouldn't.

He kept doing what he wanted to and never listened to anyone including me. I was the one who was sitting up until eleven at night to even four in the morning, and sometimes he never came home from going to the bar. I would stay up as late as I could, praying he was safe and everyone around him was too. I knew he drank and drove, and I told him he needed to stop but you know JJ; he only did what was good for him. He kept on this behavior until June 4, 2016, a day I'll never forget. He swore he wasn't drinking "very much," but I knew better.

I was cleaning the house, keeping my typical routine that I thought good wives kept. I was taking care of the house, and our three dogs, Zeus, Gunny, and Reign, making sure they were taken care of. Then as I bent down to grab the blue mop bucket, JJ mentioned he was ordering flowers for our daughter's birthday and he went silent. I looked up as I heard him making gurgling sounds and gasping for air. He started convulsing and then slid of out the brown lounge chair dropping our gray laptop as he met the floor. When he reached the floor, he was still violently convulsing. His body twitched and his eyes were wide open. I wasn't sure if he could hear me as his seizure continued. This went on for what felt like an eternity, but it was probably around three minutes or so. I placed the dogs in their crates and called 9-1-1. When the operator answered she asked if he was responsive and there was nothing. His eyes were open but cognitively he was incapable of responding. A few minutes later, he looked at me while still lying on the cold, tile floor and I said "It's okay. You're okay. I'm getting you help." He tried to get up but I made him wait until help arrived.

First Responders

Soon my house was flooded with an emergency team launching a barrage of questions at me, which I was struggling to answer. I felt as though I was having an out-of-body experience. Everything was happening so fast. I didn't know what was happening and didn't know what to do. So, I stopped everything. I pushed the cleaning supplies out of the way and called my then-brother-in-law, Morgan, and my then-mother-in-law, Cece. I let them know what was going on and if they were available to meet me at the hospital in the emergency room.

I had nothing to eat that day. I don't know if you're like me, but you will clean all day and not eat or drink anything; this is my typical schedule for when I'm cleaning. I go all out and when I'm done, then I will have a meal. You probably guessed it, I asked Cece to bring me some crackers and water. She did, and I appreciated her help. While I was eating, I sat there numb and waiting for the doctors to come in. I didn't think JJ's drinking would ever cause something like this, but it did. I HATED his drinking because it was killing him and our marriage. It was killing the family I had dreamed of having, killing everything inside of me. I hated the emergency room! I felt like the doctors and nurses were judging me for not being able to get him to stop drinking. I couldn't stand it. I hated all of it, and I wanted to get out. I wanted to be free from this hogwash. That was our third time here!

This was the third visit to the emergency room unlike any other, though. The doctors were not allowing JJ to come home but keeping him for observation since his seizure was severe, and he wasn't being honest with the hospital staff. They asked him when his last drink was, and he had had a glass of Jameson Irish Whiskey earlier that morning. His body was in shock because he hadn't had anything to drink for a few hours, which threw him into withdrawal.

The body is a beautiful organ, but when you don't take care of it, then it's going to kick your butt, so you know you need to get things in gear. JJ's body was displeased with him and wanted everything it wasn't getting. His body was the perfect representation of our marriage. It wants what it wants, but JJ will be danged if he gives it to you.

This was one of the longest weekends of my life. I went from being able to live a full life within my home to rushing between there and the hospital. My work-life balance had drastically changed in an instant. Oh my GOD! Is this my freaking life? I felt so much pressure. I had to hide his deteriorating situation from his ex-wife and ex-girlfriend, or he would lose custody or rights to his children. I had my own life to live but had no one supporting me. Everyone was supporting my drunk of a husband in the hospital and holding me to higher standards than they were for him. Pretty lousy, right?

I wasn't the one who put myself in this situation. I wasn't the one who refused to get help. On the contrary, I was the one who was reaching out, trying to get every resource I could to come in and help me. I even sat across from a social worker at the hospital because she was concerned about our situation. Come on, guys! A social worker wanted to be involved in my life because my husband wouldn't put the bottle down, and I was expected to hide this from everyone. If I didn't hide it, then there was going to be hell to pay. I knew it and had to keep myself, my dogs, and my children safe. I had to be careful about what I told anyone. I had to filter everything about our lives, and my brain was constantly in overdrive. I couldn't stop and think for myself, always pressured to put everyone and everything else in the family before me.

I met with the nurses at the hospital multiple times, but they were extremely guarded. I could usually walk into the hospital and get the answers I wanted but I couldn't here. One nurse told me JJ was there because he was going into detox, and his body couldn't handle it. Another nurse told me she didn't know why he had a seizure, and they had to complete further testing. I was beyond myself, held up in a corner of my husband's hospital room for three days, and I couldn't get any straight answers.

I didn't want to be near him, as I knew he lied about everything, and the nurses were trying to keep chaos from breaking out in the hospital room. I only wanted to know what was going on. I wanted to know why the person I loved slid to the floor and started convulsing uncontrollably. I wanted answers, that's it.

The Hospital Bed

As I watched JJ pass out and be hooked up to machines, I felt sick. I felt like I was going to vomit and pass out on the floor myself. The stress was taking a toll on my body and soul to where I could no longer manage this circus by myself. The machines beeping and going off for what seemed like every few seconds were driving me insane. I was on rotating shifts of visiting him at the hospital and going home to take care of our fur babies. They were always happy to see me, which helped as I felt like the weight of a mountain was sitting on my shoulders. I felt so guilty for leaving them at home when I visited JJ in the hospital, since he was stuck in bed.

I've heard ankle monitors for prisoners on house arrest are bad, but at least they can get up and walk around. JJ wasn't allowed to stand up without two nurses next to his sides, waiting on him hand and foot. I think he appreciated this attention but while he had the support, I had no one.

The kids stayed with us but on that particular weekend they were at their respective mother's houses. Mara, Piper, and Zoe were with Karen while Xavier was with Mia; otherwise, I would have had to help four traumatized children as well in handling their father's hospitalization. I appreciate the grace and mercy I was given during this time. When I went home, I fed, watered, and let my fur babies go out to the bathroom. We even played their favorite game, catch, which calmed my nerves.

Once I opened the door, they would race around our medium-sized backyard, a suburb of Indianapolis, surrounded by a dog-eared wood privacy fence playing chase. They loved running behind the shed and playing peek-a-boo. Sometimes I would even join in when I had the energy. We had two German Shepherds and a Belgian Malinois. Our shepherds stood tall with pointy ears, always alert and jogging the perimeter of our fence while our Belgian Malinois was either ready to pounce on an intruder or hop up for a hug. She loved getting hugs and resting her head on my chest, while the other two were quite content with barking and receiving butt scratches.

It depended on the day and how they were feeling as to what they wanted and, for the most part, they were a pretty wonderful little pack of dogs to keep me company. They were my only family when my kids weren't around, the only ones who wanted me or loved me back. They were my life, and I was grateful every day I had them. They were there for the good times and the bad. No matter how frustrated I got with them, my love was unending. They gave me a reason to get up in the morning and were soft cuddle buddies to go to sleep with.

My oldest German Shepherd, Zeus, always laid on my chest to put me to sleep. I wonder if he was only interested in taking a nap with me or if he was protecting me from something I was unaware of. Either way, he did his job. I preferred taking naps with him. He was my safe place when I had no one else I could depend on; my Zeusy boy was always there. I guess you could say he was the man in my house. He was strong, steadfast, communicative, and embodied leadership skills by training his furry siblings and loving me the only way he knew how. At least that's the void he filled for me.

When I went home to take care of them, JJ would log onto social media and complain about how he was stuck in the hospital and no one had come to visit him. This chapped my backside. He was such a drama queen and would make these posts after I hadn't been gone out of his room for more than thirty seconds. He couldn't stand being alone, and I was danged if I was in his hospital room because no one would talk to me, and then when I went home, I was shamed too. It was an uphill battle, and I was losing.

I wanted to stay home and not be around him. If he was going to complain on social media about me, I might as well have stayed home. But JJ would call me and ask when I was coming back. I wanted this weekend to be over. I wanted my marriage to be over. I was tired of all the hospital trips and was too young to be dealing with this, but I had zero support from the people who knew about the situation. These people were JJ's blood relatives and told me I had no business kicking my husband out of the house. That's because they didn't want him in their houses, dealing with his choices.

Back home

Soon after JJ got home from the hospital, he swore he wouldn't put me through something like this again. I already had a girls' trip scheduled to go on, and he encouraged me to go. His family, on the other hand, said I was being irresponsible in leaving my husband home by himself.

Really? He was the drunk, and they had the audacity to tell me I was the one who was being irresponsible. The last time I checked, I was his wife and not his mommy. It wasn't my job to control what he was doing. He was choosing to drink, smoke, and chew tobacco. This was his choice, and I needed a vacation. I needed an opportunity to clear my head and get away. If I didn't leave, I was going to file for divorce. The only reason I would be staying was our four children. I wanted to make sure they were safe because I didn't trust JJ because of his choices.

JJ kept waking up and telling me he was having a recurring dream that he got in a car accident while he was taking our kids somewhere and they all died. At this point, I never let him drive our kids anywhere. I made sure I was ready to go whenever they wanted to go somewhere, and I supervised him. I wasn't going to lose my kids and I, for dang sure, wasn't going to put myself in a position where I was going to have to call my kids' mothers to tell them they've been in an accident.

I sacrificed a lot because JJ wouldn't quit drinking, but you know what, it was worth it. It was worth it to me to keep my kids safe. Someone in our house had to be the grown-up, and that person always had to be me.

4

CHOICES

While I was home, I'd use this time to think about life and where I was headed. Let's be honest; I didn't want to head back to the hospital anytime soon. I didn't mind being there, but good grief, my husband was a blockhead who landed himself in this mess to begin with. He'd been given the tools and support to break the cycle of alcohol abuse and had the choice to stop. Before you throw this book across the room because you want to defend an alcoholic, hear me out.

Everyone in life has a choice. I had a choice to stay in a relationship and love my alcoholic husband through this, and I did. Looking back now, I should have left and focused on my relationships with my children's mothers, but I didn't feel safe enough to do this then because I was being mentally abused daily by my husband. He manipulated my environment to be full of confusion where I didn't feel I could approach a friend with what I was going through. I felt powerless in an unimaginable situation. So, I stuck next to him and never reached out to them. I had to protect myself because no one else would do it. At one point, I had a decent relationship with their moms, but I let that go. It wasn't safe for me to be involved with them, especially with what happened when no one else could see.

And, yes, I said mothers because my ex-husband is a serial adulterer. We all know and have compared histories about this man. All our histories are similar, except he twists history to meet his manipulative desires. I don't believe he has ever spoken the truth about either of these women or what he did to them, and the truth will never be known because he believes his lies. Nothing is a surprise to us or our children anymore. We thought he'd become a better man when he married me, but that fantasy was flushed down the toilet right next to Cinderella. Fairy tales don't exist when you're married to an abuser, but nightmares do.

When married to or defending an alcoholic, I would suggest you keep a few things in mind. The number one reminder is their drinking is NEVER your fault. Please read this again: Their drinking is never your fault. My experience with an alcoholic has taught me how to not only have compassion for myself but those within my family. Alcoholism is a family disease, and it doesn't affect only one person.

My ex-husband pretended he had stopped drinking after being discharged from the hospital. Maybe he did, but I'll never know the truth. I prayed with every fiber of my being he would achieve sobriety and become sort of like the man I fell in love with. I saw a glimmer of happiness floating in front of me, but I was nervous if I should reach out and grab it. And I did! I grabbed that little glimmer of hope, as our lives seemed like they were getting better for the following six months.

One way to happiness was when my husband purchased a bike so we could ride together. Our town included many beautiful bike paths we spent time enjoying. I loved riding my bike next to him and was extremely happy he was taking steps to make our family stronger and taking his health seriously. I laughed more that summer than I could remember in a long time. This was the fun guy I married; I was glad to have him back. His smile lit up my world, and I didn't care he had chewing tobacco stuck in his teeth. What mattered was I had a chance to get the one I loved back and restore what we had before.

This lasted for the summer, and then it quickly faded away. When late fall and early winter arrived, he seemed to have returned to that shell of a man I saw lying in the hospital bed. I didn't know him anymore, and this would be one of the last summers we spent time together with any type of authentic emotion, even if it was fleeting. In December of 2016, I wanted out of our marriage. I could see I was the only one who was putting forth any effort, except there were four very important people I didn't want to leave behind, my children, so I stayed.

Around Christmas, our twin girls came over for a visit and went shopping with JJ. He took them into the jewelry store where they helped him pick out an "upgraded" wedding ring and a necklace that read "I love you" for me. He said it was from the girls, and any little thing for me from them I was happy to receive. I'm down to earth and don't require expensive gifts, but it is nice to be appreciated. These gifts were the breadcrumbs that kept me in my marriage. I deserved more but to JJ, I was only a possession to be owned, and my daughters were a pawn he used to get what he wanted.

All this happiness was short-lived. The pretty gifts I got at Christmas soon faded into darkness, as I caught him drinking again in February of 2017, and my heart sank. He blamed his choice on me and said, "It's your fault I drink." I had never forced a bottle into his hand, nor is it my fault he wouldn't address the pains deep within him. His trauma was not my responsibility.

He lost his father in August of 2011 and refused to seek professional counseling for his grief. His Grandma even offered her connection at the funeral home where her husband had been buried, but he wouldn't accept any help. He expected me to listen to him while he was three sheets to the wind.

I couldn't do it. I couldn't heal the pains I had from watching my beloved father-in-law and best friend fade from this life and couldn't continue to counsel my husband. I sat for two months in a deep depression, doing nothing except when my kids came for a visit. I kept the house tidy enough for them; otherwise, I didn't care about anything. I missed my friend. I missed our conversations and the jokes he used to tell. I missed the person I could be myself around him, especially since I didn't have a relationship with my father.

Though this time was hard, I had to pull myself off the couch to get it together, as someone had to keep our family afloat. Since my husband was drowning his sorrows in whisky and vodka, I had to take the lead. I had to be the man and the woman in our house, the dad and the mom. I also had to pay for everything since he refused to help me; our family wasn't his problem anymore.

The second thing I suggest you remember is you are NEVER in control of their drinking. I can almost guarantee if my ex-husband was reading this right now, he would be irate. When I would push back and remind him his drinking was not my fault, he would get heated. This is something I would encourage you to do. Stand up for yourself if you are in a safe place. Gather a group of friends and family to execute an intervention.

Thirdly, I would encourage you to keep this in mind. You cannot control how much alcohol an alcoholic purchases. If you're anything like me, you might be so desperate when they have times they seem sober and drive away. You ransack your house looking for every bottle you can find and find every bottle they have hidden or not. In this process, you are more likely to lose your own sanity in my opinion; I know because I've been there. I was the one who scoured the house and found fourteen different types of alcohol bottles during one night's mission. JJ went as far as blaming his friend at the police department as to why he has several bottles of whiskey stored in the back of his black Toyota 4-Runner. Right, bud, like a police officer is going to call you to assist. After all, his son was "out of control and drinking" because he's in high school. Why would he have chosen to send the alcohol to our house, and he'll be coming to retrieve it later on?

I didn't believe a word he said. He was so pitiful, he helped himself to my wine and blamed it on our dog, Zeus. He explained how Zeus opened the refrigerator and pulled my wine out and broke the bottle. At this point, my husband was fishing for an emotional reaction from me. He wanted me to explode because I couldn't sit down, relax, and enjoy a glass of wine after a hard day's work. Nope! I didn't react; I only responded with "Okay."

I'm going to let you in on a little-known secret. My dog can open doors, but he has never opened the refrigerator door. Dogs don't have thumbs, and my refrigerator door lacked a handle because my husband refused to attach it. So, I asked, "How could Zeus possibly have opened the door when there was no way for him to physically do this?" Bingo, you guessed it! He didn't! This was another fictional story from the miserable tales of an alcoholic with a bias in perception.

His "truths" were the only ones that mattered. If I were to challenge him, it would throw him into a rage. He would slam doors, gaslight me, and mentally or physically assault me, in one way or another, so, for me, it was best to stay calm. This is how I survived the trauma and how God protected me in the moments I wanted to lash out. He kept me calm and steady and was the rock I stood on because nothing else could protect me as He can. I would mentally kneel in these moments and be covered with the wings of my guardian angel. During these moments, I would stare as my tongue was bridled, and nothing came out. I stood and observed JJ until he left my presence to make sure I was safe.

He thought I believed him, but I was buying time until the truth came out. I knew something was off but what?

5

SEALED

After the door shut behind JJ, and I knew he would never walk into my house again as my husband, I sat for a moment and listened to the deafening silence. This silence had been there every night I wailed on the ripped leather, couch crying out to God and asking, "Why?" Why isn't my life turning out the way I had hoped? Why are the prayers I've been praying similar to a broken record not being answered? At this moment, I permitted myself to be riled. I screamed at the top of my lungs as I slammed my fists into the ugly leather couch JJ had to have. He needed to have an ugly, cold, brown couch that matched his dead soul.

An ugly, cold, brown couch that mirrored the lack of relationships he would ever come in contact with. The couch was as dead as he was because neither of them had a soul at this point. The couch had massive holes ripped into the leather, and the seams stitched together, holding the entirety of the couch together burst open. You could see a shell of where a couch stood, but nothing was salvage-able. This couch was similar to JJ's soul, for you could see a man who had trained himself to appear empathetic and comforting but, like the couch, his innards were exposed. There was nothing inside of this man. There was no soft place to fall, no comfort, no fluff, no emotions. He was just an ugly couch ripped open with Jameson Irish Whiskey bottles shoved in the side of the furniture, and he would take a swig when needed to numb his pain. When life got too real, or I needed him to be the husband he promised me he would be, he would numb out.

I looked around the house and at that moment, I decided there was nothing I wanted from him. I tried to fix what was broken but he wanted no part of it, so I took responsibility for something I didn't break. He promised me he would have children with me or adopt if he couldn't, due to his having cancer, but he never followed through on this, even though we talked with our children about adopting. This was part of his con to get me into marrying him, and it worked. I got the better end of the deal, as I was blessed with mothering the children he never wanted. I thank God for them every day. In a way, I got the children I've always dreamed of having, as he was the nincompoop who was too blind to see the gifts standing in front of him.

The other issue at hand was JJ also promised to pay the $40,000.00 tax bill he incurred when he received an inheritance of $453,000.00 when his father passed away. His dad stated this money was supposed to be used for "his grandchildren's college funds, our retirement, a small family trip, and the rest was for savings." This never happened though because Mitch's wishes were not respected. JJ said the tax bill was "taken care of." Well, nine years later, I found out he had not taken care of this bill. He simply hired a team of lawyers to file paperwork. stating he couldn't pay the bill. This only created more issues for me because I made $11,000.00 dollars less than JJ per year, and he stuck me with the bill, on top of me paying for the entirety of our household, except for our cell phone and grocery bills. Let's be honest: The only reason he paid the phone bill was to keep tabs on me and the groceries because I put him on a $20.00 weekly allowance, as that's all I had left after paying all the bills. This created a huge problem when the Internal Revenue Service wanted their money because I had nothing left to give them.

JJ refused to call them or set up a plan because he said he had "taken care of the bill." Since he said it was paid, then he felt he had nothing to worry about. However, I knew better. I continued calling the IRS until I got someone to take my phone call. I waived my rights to have the previous lawyers speak for me and found out JJ had used the lawyers to keep me from speaking to the IRS. So even if I would have called about this situation much sooner, I wouldn't have been allowed to talk to them because of the paperwork he filed.

I didn't know this was the man I married, a man who took $453,000.00 and put it in an account where I couldn't touch it. I also found out he cashed out my $40,000.00 in retirement money and spent it. He also received another check for $50,000.00 he never told me about and where the money is, I have no clue. This is the man I married. A man who squanders money and uses women to get what he wants and lacks any decency at all. I wonder what my late father-in-law would say if he was here to witness this; I can only imagine what he would say.

During that time, JJ lied to me about the bill being paid. He spent money on a Red 1969 Dodge Cornett R/T Convertible he said was inherited from his father—it was not—five tickets to the Notre Dame BCS College Championship football game in Orlando, Florida, including the Fan Zone, airline tickets, hotel, and rental car. He also took a "business trip" out to Las Vegas, Nevada, where he went to the casino, took several trips within the United States, purchased college classes he never finished, and gave $25,000 to his sister. Additionally, he purchased furniture, bought suits, supposedly paid child support, and took multiple trips to places like Sky Zone for the kids. He had a hay day with all this money but decided he wasn't going to pay the bill and left it for me to pay. His CPA was also at fault because he assured me this bill was paid when it wasn't. Unfortunately, he died of cancer about two months after he filed our taxes so he never admitted his wrongdoing. I've learned my lesson: don't trust CPAs who are friends of your husband and his family.

Overall, I've learned that JJ was never a husband or a good man to me. He was a man-child who needed his mouth wiped, his bedtime set, and the house cleaned for him since he was too incompetent to do it himself. He never wanted a wife. He wanted a mommy he could have sex with, abuse, and manipulate. Perhaps he needed the love he never received as a child. At least, this is what he told me when we were married, saying he had to be the man of the house growing up and since he was out of his childhood home, he didn't want to be a man at all.

I wish he would have passed me by instead of marrying me. I could have done without all the evil, torment, and abuse he has inflicted on me. I didn't deserve this treatment regardless of what happened to him growing up. This is not what I signed up for and I'm looking forward to continuing my life without this chaos.

6

FORGIVENESS

I was thrust into a darkness I never wanted to know. The darkness was cold, damp, and had a musty smell. The smell your laundry room walls might wreak of after there's been a flood.

The darkness I sat in smelled worse than that, more like a rotting corpse with puss spewing out of it. The kind you might have seen on the show *Chicago Fire*. The man's body was swollen, and the maggots were consuming his lifeless body. This was the type of darkness I was living in, the reality of my marriage.

I had a choice like many of us do. I could choose to acknowledge that my husband was never capable of loving me and only entered into a marriage to meet his selfish desires, or I could hold onto the pain and let it define my life. When we experience pain, it is meant to be a part of our life, but it's not meant to define us forever.

When you experience pain, sit with it. Hold it in your body and process the experience that has taken place, then do your best to let it go. You may have to do this again and again. As you do this, it'll get easier, and the pain will be less excruciating.

You can forgive on your time and on your terms, just don't take so long that your life passes you by. Don't miss the next chapter in your life because you're busy holding onto the last chapter. The old chapter is over, and you have a gorgeous life waiting right in front of you, so go live it. You don't want to miss out on life and the purpose you were sent here to fulfill because of unresolved drama.

I would even encourage you to pray for those who've hurt you. I know this probably sounds wild, but it can help. The reason the person who hurt you did this in the first place is because they may have an empty hole within them that needs healing. I know because the person who hurt me is the one who needs the most healing.

I spent the latter years of my marriage observing JJ die. He wasn't dying in the literal sense, but he was in the mind, body, and spirit. He may have seemed like a confident, humorous, adventurous, friendly man but I knew the truth about him. A truth that probably no one else could see. I don't think anyone else could see it because they didn't see him the way I did. They lacked clarity whereas I spent over a decade with him, so I've seen many sides of JJ that he won't choose to show others who live outside the walls of our house.

Everything he felt inside, he was projecting onto me. The hate, loneliness, unworthiness, silence, and darkness, all of this defined his internal being. He never wanted it to be exposed except when it came to me, where he was enraged, which is what I saw often. When I looked at him, I see a scared, lost, little boy who wasn't held when he needed to be. I see a man who couldn't parent because he didn't know how to truly be there for someone else besides himself.

I see a man who had so much potential to give the most beautiful gift to this world. The gift he would give is his true, vulnerable self. Sure, he was skilled at mathematics, problem-solving and humor but his real self is the gift. This was lost because somewhere along the line in his short life, a tragedy happened. Something happened so terribly that he buried it deep within his soul. This secret he carries is killing the person he was meant to be. For this reason, no one will ever get to know the real JJ. He was too afraid to be real and vulnerable. When he was vulnerable, he was in a place of exposure, and this was too risky, especially for him. So, I prayed for him. I still pray for JJ because when someone is so dead inside, they're numb to the world, and only God can get to them if they open the "door" to Him.

JJ isn't who he could be. The truth is I'll never know who he could be. When he was chatting with me one time, he slipped and mentioned something, but I don't know whether this was true or something he said to throw me off. I don't feel it would be fair to share, but my instinct tells me I'm correct. The thing he slipped and told me was probably true, and he dropped his guard when he told me. This doesn't excuse the pain and terror he had inflicted upon me nor give him or anyone else the right to cause me excruciating pain because they've been through hell. Two wrongs don't make a right; my parents taught me this. Hurting someone is never justifiable. Forgiving them though is a gift you can give to them and yourself.

Forgiveness allows you to release yourself from a situation the devil meant for destruction, as I know God will use it for good. I can at least say this in my situation. At times, it seemed like God left me and when I looked, I couldn't find Him in the mess. This wasn't true. He was walking with me in my mess, and I couldn't feel Him because He was walking with me. He was watching my steps and guiding me, making sure I stayed on the right path through the fire I was walking through. He had to make sure I didn't stop in hell. He had to make sure I kept going and didn't give up.

The pain JJ caused me hurt so badly that I wanted to stop. I wanted to die and didn't want to keep going. I wanted to stay in bed and wait for God to take me, but He didn't. He put people in my life, as He may with yours, who motivates you to keep going. On the days I wanted to quit, my daughter Piper would send me text messages, or my son Xavier would send me an update on how his athletic achievements were progressing. This kept me focused on what mattered. They did this without any communication from me on how I was doing. They just sent the messages, which turned my day around. I missed life with them, missed having them over every other weekend.

The pain didn't matter, but my children did. The fact that my husband cheated on me and then said his affair partner was threatening to burn my house down, where I was living with my two dogs, didn't matter. I know from his behavioral track record he was the one who said this. So, I filed a police report detailing his and her information with the officer, but still, this is not what matters. This threat kept me from sleeping at night; therefore, I moved out of the house. I feared for my life, my fur babies' lives, and the lives of my neighbors.

I survived the abuse and by helping you through this book, I'm overcoming it. God kept me going so I could reach back and help those that need it. I'm here to let you know that the situation you're in or might be in is not the end. This is not the last fight you're going to go up against. This is the fight that will challenge you to become a better person. This is your moment, the time for you to rise up and stand on your own two feet and say enough is enough. Your abuser doesn't own you, nor does your situation.

You can get out if you choose to get out of an abusive relationship. You can stand and fight, or you can wait it out and let your abuser leave as I did; either way, this moment is yours. You will define this moment. You are stronger than your situation. You are the Rocky in your life, and your comeback story is waiting on you … Step up, rise up, and become your own hero.

7

FAILURES

Have you ever failed at something? Have you felt as though you did your best, putting your best efforts forward, and it didn't work out? I get it. When I was packing my house up and donating things to Goodwill, since I no longer had space for it, my mother said I was tenacious. She said this in the middle of a conversation we were having because I don't quit on people until I've fully made up my mind to walk away. I make sure I put every effort into that relationship, taking everything that has occurred and dissecting it. I make one hundred percent sure I put my full effort into it. I make sure there's not something I could have done better to fix the situation.

I do this all the time on a day-to-day basis. Some might call me an over-thinker ... Well, I am. I dissect and overanalyze everything. It's a blessing and a curse, although this approach allows me to reflect and grow in my day-to-day activities. It allows me to see the big picture and focus on the microscopic parts of my life, to see where I can grow.

You see, failure is not the end but the beginning in my opinion. It took me years to arrive at this mindset shift, about six years to be exact to change my way of thinking. I would look at other people through rose-colored glasses, thinking they had everything I wanted. I compared myself to everything they had and criticized myself, wondering why I didn't have it. Why can't I get some of that romantic love?

The truth is, I wasn't ready for a blessing of this caliber. I was consistently comparing myself to others, which wasn't doing anything but shrinking my gifts into a place of non-existence. God couldn't work when I was walking around with discontent, questioning my maker as to why He hadn't blessed me with something yet.

Think about a two-year-old watching you put hot sauce on your mac-n-cheese. This is so freaking delicious. I ate some last night. BUT then your toddler throws a temper tantrum because you won't meet her wants or want her to have the same thing. First of all, any parent with a conscience knows this would be the worst possible choice. This is a heat an adult can handle but not a toddler. You observe her as she rolls around on the floor screaming because she knows she wants this hot sauce, but she doesn't understand you are protecting her.

This is kind of the same thing when God doesn't bless us as we think we should. When we are crying out in pain to God while sitting on the couch during prayer time, begging Him to please, please give us the blessing, as tears stream down your face, but He knows better. He can see the bigger picture. He knows this will be our "hot sauce." He knows we are not ready for it; therefore, it's not our blessing to be had. This blessing belongs to someone else who is ready for it.

So, the next time you see someone with something you've been begging God for, stop and consider why it isn't yours. Consider why God decided it was for someone else and not you. Maybe you have been shrinking yourself to fit into a box He didn't design you for, and He's waiting for you to step into your purpose. Maybe He's getting ready to make your situation so uncomfortable because you've outgrown it, and you'll be moving elsewhere. Consider His protection and what's going on behind the scenes. Maybe, just maybe, God has a blessing so awesome that it will blow your mind. Maybe the thing you've been praying for will actually be a burden, and God can't bear to watch you suffer so He won't allow it to pass through His hands. Everything that touches you first has to pass through His hands. He decides if it's for us or not.

Think about this for a moment: my ex-husband, JJ, promised me the world. He promised me a baby in the biological or adoptive form, but this blessing never came. God knew it wasn't good for us. He knew it reeeeeeaaallly wasn't good for me. I cried, begged, pleaded, and took on more jobs to earn the money to be ready for this person I loved so much that never arrived. I had names picked out for them; I wanted a son and a daughter. I actually wanted to adopt four kids and have two, and at least part of this dream happened. To be honest, working in a grocery store helped trim down the number of children I wanted. I call those children birth control because WOW, did some of those parents let their kids run wild in a store. If you ever want a show, grab a coffee and go to the grocery store to watch the kids. It'll educate you on who's running the house.

Anyways, I did everything possible in my control so I could have more children. Unfortunately and fortunately, the day came when I accepted this was never going to happen with JJ. It was a cool day in January. I vaguely remember talking to God and telling Him if He didn't want me to be a mother to take this want away from me. He didn't take it immediately, but over time, it disappeared. He allowed me to grieve this loss, as though I was grieving the death of someone who was here on earth but never was. I didn't realize I could love someone so much who was never actually here.

Once I made peace with God's decision, I was relieved it was gone. I was happy because I could focus on the children who were already chosen for me. I didn't like sharing them, but it wasn't so bad. I'd spend every waking moment with them if I could, but that wouldn't be realistic. I was thankful for every moment I got and that was the plan, as of this moment, that God had for me. He knew if I had a biological child, my life would so much worse.

He knew I would have been trapped with JJ, and my child would have been used as a pawn just as their older siblings have been. I didn't want this for my children. I didn't want them riding in the car with a drunk who crashed into other people's cars and didn't stop. I didn't even want this for my children, here on earth already entrusted to me. It was my duty to protect them, and that's what I was going to do.

Does this sound familiar? I'm protecting my children just as God has protected me, His child. Just like He's protecting you if you consider yourself His child. He knows what He's doing. He has the big picture right in front of Him, and we can only see a glimpse of what's in front of Him.

This right here is why I don't think failure is actually failing anymore. My mindset changed, opening me up to a world where I stopped looking at all the what-ifs and started seeing the maybes. I started seeing who I am and my purpose. I started stepping out in faith and trusting each step was ordered for me to walk. I took each step and trusted God had my best interest at heart and looked at the opportunity that was available right in front of me. I was ready to step but this time ... I JUMPED! I jumped at the opportunities in front of me. And you know what, I finally feel like His blessings are upon me.

Yes, I finally feel His blessings upon me. So maybe you're not failing, friend; maybe God is testing you to see how serious you are before He moves you. Maybe He's seeing if you fully trust Him and how you will respond when He does bless you. Trust Him! I'm living proof that life does get better. He has blessed me with a wonderful teaching position and the finances to make my life better. He's got us!

Your life may not be where you want it to be, but I believe you'll get there. He's testing you and waiting for you to have unmovable faith to bless you and move you forward.

8

HEALING

Healing is an extraordinary idea, one that requires great focus to become better. In my opinion, it also requires courage as we address the things that have crippled us in our past. To heal is to break free from the bondage that has kept us trapped and unable to break free.

According to Merriam-Webster's Dictionary, healing is defined as the act or process of curing or restoring health. The process of getting well. Healing. ("Heal." Merriam-Webster.com Dictionary, Merriam-Webster, https://www.merriam-webster.com/dictionary/heal. Accessed 16 Mar. 2024.)

I agree with both of these definitions. In order to allow me to get on a path of healing, I had to first lose myself. I had to enter into a relationship where someone took complete and total advantage of me. He dehumanized me to make himself feel better about the torture he had been putting me through.

I don't know about you, but if I were to hate myself this much when I woke up in the morning that I wanted to destroy other lives, I'd rather stay in bed and drink myself to death. Unfortunately, this may be the life some of us have led. I know it's the life I lived because it was forced upon me.

JJ used to say I was the best woman he had ever met. He never thought he would ever find anyone like me. At this time, I didn't know he was love -bombing me, but I do now. Love bombing is the act of showing someone a lot of love or positive attention in order to make them do what you want ("Love Bombing." Dictionary.cambridge.org, Dictionary, Cambridge, https://dictionary.cambridge.org/us/dictionary/english/love-bombing.Accessed 16 Mar. 2024.) When he met me, I was in a place of healing, but I didn't have the resources available that I do now. He interrupted my life when I was helping a co-worker get out of an unsafe environment, taking advantage of this situation by butting into my life. If I would have had the boundaries I do now back then, I wouldn't be writing this book.

I know because I'm a completely different woman than I was two years ago. I've had the courage to seek out a mental health professional to help me sort out every emotion I've encountered. He has also helped me understand what took place in my marriage was not my fault, and it has never been something I needed to take responsibility for. I'm not saying I'm perfect or I haven't made a mistake, but the abuse was a conscious choice JJ made, and that is one hundred percent on him.

He invited evil into our lives, dancing with it hand in hand as he purposefully broke my spirit. He chose to marry me, promising to have children, biological or by adopting, and he kept pressing me to purchase a bigger house and became angry when I refused to stretch my already thinned-out finances. Slander became his blame game, as he carefully crafted lies to make it my fault so people would feel sorry for him in a life he created. Nope, he's no victim; it's on him. He made his bed, and he can sleep in it.

When I was growing up, I always thought I had to be the best to a fault. At the age of nine, my parents stopped correcting me about my grades because I was a perfectionist. I even bought a book on how not to be a perfectionist. Yikes! How many nine-year-olds do you know that are focused on not being a perfectionist?

This was the world I was living in. This focus was self-inflicted, as I didn't like making mistakes or being thought of as weak, so I overcompensated. I tried to be the best role model out there for all my younger cousins, wanting them to see I was "good." I wanted them to see I was worthy, but I never actually received the validation I was seeking. It's really sad I was seeking external validation from them in the first place, and not getting it. I should have been seeking it from God but as a young child, the drum of society's approval was louder than God.

At this age, God was this skinny, old man in a giant chair with a notebook, writing down every single time I fudged up. I used to imagine when I died, He was going to tell me how big of a screw-up I was. Maybe this is where my fault for perfectionism came from. I'll never know. What I do know is I judged God wrongly. I messed up in life, and I'm going to own it.

I messed up because my unhealed heart couldn't allow God to love me. I couldn't accept His love because I didn't think I was good or worthy enough to be loved. The popular kids at school didn't love me, the kid with a learning disability, so why would I be good enough for God?

I've spent numerous hours forming a relationship with my father, a father I know will love me no matter the label I have on myself or the person I am. I know He will love me even though I thought higher of myself than I should have. When I'm measuring myself against God, it's like I'm the clay who's telling the potter if He can love me or not. I'm telling Him what to do without half the information He has.

Umm, the last time I checked, the clay is not in charge. In college, I stayed in the school dorms for two summer sessions and would go into the art building late at night. I did this so I could have the pottery studio all to myself and wouldn't be bothered. These were the days before YouTube or any other type of apps. Go ahead and laugh! I know it seems like centuries ago, but it has not been that long ago. I enjoyed sitting in silence as the clay would be carefully molded between my fingers and the wheel danced in circles. I took careful measurements to make sure my sculptures were sturdy and could withstand the test of time, especially wanting them to withstand the heat in the kiln.

If I had to guess, I bet God designed us in a similar way. He knew He needed us here to fulfill some type of destiny; otherwise, we probably wouldn't be here. I know I was specifically designed to endure the marriage I went through, as He built me with His strength and courage. He created me with the ability to heal by getting to know Him personally. He designed me with the strength of a warrior, even though my battle cry had been silenced. The cry is within me, and the hellfire I was put through was so I'd remember the woman I was sent here to be. He chose me just as He chose you.

When I imagined marriage, I imagined it was my husband and me against the world. It was the two of us who were going to show the world what it was to be dedicated to each other, and love wasn't only a word to be tossed around. Well, hindsight is 100/100 right? Okay, maybe this is how I feel in my case.

I've gotten to look back and learn from the history I experienced when married to Satan's son.

No, he wasn't born Satan's son, but the actions he took against me created this dynamic in our marriage. He is still God's son, even though he has turned his back on God by the way he's living ... He's making it clear that he lives for pleasure and to fulfill his sick and twisted desires. He doesn't care who he tramples on to get what he wants. So, it was up to me; I decided I was going to be the one who showed others how to love as Jesus does.

Loving people as Jesus does was my overall goal for my marriage. I'm someone who always has a list of achievements I want to accomplish, and this one was at the top of my list. At that time, I was a wife and a stepmother. I didn't want a garbage marriage that typically came along with being in a stepfamily, so I set the goal to become the best wife and mother I could be by loving my family.

This meant loving my husband even when he was making asinine choices. During my marriage, I didn't realize I was being abused. I only came to realize this after we separated, and the trauma bond he had forced upon me was severed. Once this was broken, then I was able to reconnect with my body and brain, understanding what I had endured.

Before we were separated, I knew God could change my situation if He wanted to, but if He wasn't going to change it or my husband, then He must need to change my heart. During this time, I attend a mission at my church, which softly cracked open the door to my heart. I was ready to learn more about Jesus.

This mission took me through the ways it does and does not look to be a Christian. The deacon leading this seemed pretty perfect until he revealed his own struggles he experienced in life. He explained the Bible didn't always make sense to him, and it wasn't just some old book that should be sitting on our shelves. He encouraged us to pick it up and start with a simple chapter. A chapter we could easily connect to and start understanding who God really is, not who we decided He is. This was a turning point in my life.

At that time in my life, I was working five jobs trying to make ends meet. My husband had inherited money from the death of his father, but I didn't have access to this money. The only time he gave me any money was when the kids came over and he had me take them out.

I liked this because I got to spend time with them and grow our relationships more, but it was money for fun. I was the one who was solely responsible for all the bills in our house because JJ refused to help. When I told him I didn't have money to pay the electric bill, JJ said "Fine, then I guess we just won't have any electricity." I didn't have any room on my credit card because it was maxed out from other bills, and my bank account held enough to pay for gas and food. I would have to decide which bills to skip so our electricity didn't get shut off. JJ was stingy with his money, and his actions broke my trust. I was a single wife and stepmother helping my family while he sat on his rear, drinking whiskey and watching television.

I decided to start praying and asking God to change my heart because I wanted out. I wanted out of this loveless marriage I was in, but I didn't believe in divorce or quitting on people. I didn't want to take the easy way out. My perspective on this matter has changed since then, but during my marriage, I was trying to love JJ through his pain. Ironic, because he weaponized this pain and used it against me. The very reasons he decided he loved me and wanted me to be a wife to him and a stepmother to his children were the very reasons he ended up hating me. It was the reason he justified torturing me.

When JJ and I would spend time together, he would complement me and tell me how much he appreciated my soft touch, how he appreciated my care and concern for his children, or how fun I was to be around. I was carefree and fun! I would spin around the kitchen and dance while the kids watched me, but this happiness soon faded. He said their moms used to be like this too, but they changed as well. Man, I wish I would have pushed into this comment deeper from him. What can I say besides I was smitten, especially with the four, beautiful, little faces that greeted me when I came to visit, so I got distracted when he made this comment.

Those little faces and hearts wrecked my world for the better. I never knew I could love anyone as much as I did when I looked at them. God worked miracles when he sent me Mara, Xavier, Piper, and Zoe. These little kids were the exact reason I met JJ. I met them because I needed them, and they needed me. In their own ways, they taught me how to be a better person and live with a new perspective, and I know they will be some of the best teachers I've ever had. They're wonderful people, and I'm so happy to have had them in my life.

Fast forward to being married for seven years, and God was working on my heart. I wasn't always the easiest person to live with, and I know I could be hardheaded at times, but that was me. God needed to fix this little heart issue and worked where I'd let Him in my heart. He will knock on your heart, but He won't force his way in. He only wants to be in the hearts that openly accept Him. I guess you could say He had to wait for my free will invitation to activate. I wouldn't want anyone to be forced to love me, and I'm guessing God sees it the same way as well.

He patiently waited for me to open my heart to Him, and once I allowed God in, I started praying for my children's mothers. I know, it probably sounds wild that I would pray for them, but I felt called to do so. Through this heart work, God allowed me to "see" from their perspectives. He allowed me to have a view from their "seat." He let me see and sample what it would be like to share my children with a stepmother. He let me see how their lives did not go as planned. This made my perspective more receptive to what they might be experiencing. I read many books that helped me understand what it would feel like to be a mother to share my children with another woman. A woman who is standing in the position they once held.

I'd rather drink vinegar. If you've ever drank vinegar, you know it tastes awful. I bet that's what it feels like for a mother to have to share her children with a stepmother. So, I changed my position and showed them compassion, even if they didn't know that's what I was doing. I knew, and that's what mattered to me the most.

The second heart step God took was loving my husband unconditionally. He called me to love the drunken fool passed out in his chair. I would have liked to meet this directive with a hard pass and walk out of this chaos. However, I took my wedding vows seriously. I'm taking a wild guess that maybe some of you have been in this same position where God was asking you to do something for Him. He was asking you to humble yourself, but you thought to yourself this was nuts and told God it was not going to fit in your schedule. Try me another day God because I'm booked today. Gotta go! Bye! Peace! Exit stage left.

Yea, I totally get it. I was DONE with this drunk! I had sat next to JJ on three different hospital stays because he wouldn't put the bottle down. He was infuriating! Even so, I was called to forgive him.

Forgiving him is not something that came easily to me. I was the one who took care of the house, kids, and dogs, plus I worked five freaking jobs. Yet, he was drunk and passed out in his lounge chair regularly. We weren't even intimate for about three to four years of our marriage, and I figured he was being stupid with other women. However, I chose not to go there because I didn't have proof, and no one had the guts to come forward to tell me the truth. Since we've divorced, people came out of the woodwork to tell me what was going on. It's interesting how that happens. Maybe next time, instead of remaining silent, you grab on to some courage and help a woman out, no matter how hard it may be, and bring the proof with you.

I continued with what I was asked to do, and I learned to forgive him. I learned to love as Jesus did. Whenever I had an unforgiving thought pop into my head, I held it captive and weighed where it came from. I'd process it and let it go. This approach I continued with for years and in the end, I was the one who ended up changed. I learned how to honor God by honoring my family and became the wife I always wanted to be.

Ultimately, this helped when my family imploded with the divorce. When my prayers were finally answered, it sounded something like this:

"Hey, God, it's me again. I'm giving up and giving JJ back. I don't want him anymore. I don't want to feel like this, and I'm tired. I'm tired of him leaving every other weekend and telling me he's going out with his guy friends. I'm done, God. I have nothing left to give anymore. I must either choose me or him, and I don't choose him anymore. Go after him, God. Go see what he's doing. Go find out who he's with. I know he's lying, and I'm not here for it anymore. I'll stay until you let me know it's time to go. In Jesus's name, I pray. Amen."

From this moment on, it was God and me together, fighting as one. I asked God for someone to have the strength and courage to reach out and tell me what JJ was doing. I knew it wasn't good as often as he was leaving, but a part of me was okay with him leaving because that meant he wasn't hurting me when he was gone. I got to be at peace with my dogs, Gunny and Reign, and we got to enjoy life without JJ's constant abuse, torment, and mind games. It was peaceful when he was gone, and I didn't miss him at all. I was glad he was gone, and some days it would have been better if he walked out the door when he went to see his affair partners and never came back. I mean he hurried up and got up before me on Saturdays to rush out the door to go hiking. This was something I suggested we do together, but he used this time away from me to facilitate cheating behavior. It's his loss. The money he spent avoiding me on the trips was the money he was stealing from our family. He didn't deserve me or our family.

During this time, I found the healing process to be challenging and helpful. I chose to have the courage to heal what was broken within me. The brokenness that led me to marry a coward who said he loved his family with his whole heart. Yea, more like he loves you as long as you give him money and focus all your attention on him, only. He got jealous when I went to the kids' events, and he wasn't there, saying it made him "look bad."

When sitting in the quiet, I allowed myself to feel all the hurt I had trapped in my body. This wasn't specific to my marriage but to my entire life. I dug up every dirty emotion I had shoved deep into my gut, promising I'd never look at it again. Sometimes I'd write or draw my feelings out, and then sometimes I gave myself permission to cry myself to sleep. This helped me make peace with everything I'd been through, especially when I addressed my abandonment issues and let things go. The things I once clung to because I was fearful of losing them are no longer hard for me to let go of now. I release things from my grip and know once I don't feel for them anymore, they were no longer meant for me.

This is the way I felt about my husband when I gave him back to God. I outgrew him, and we both knew it, so he moved on to a new supply, a male school resource officer who liked flipping the camera off and one or both posted it on Facebook. This must have been why he behaved like a prick when he walked into my house to move JJ out. Apparently, he was the only "friend" who could help him move out but it felt like JJ was using him to intimidate me.

The officers body language worried me and I didn't trust he had good intentions. When I asked to see his badge, it was covered with a hoodie since he was dressed in plain clothes and he was ill-mannered. Next, I asked for dispatch's number. I wanted to verify the badge number was authentic; he spit the number out so fast I couldn't hear it. This gave me an uneasy feeling and I asked him to repeat the number. This time I was able to catch all the numbers, still I didn't feel comfortable because officers are supposed to make sure citizens feel safe and secure and he did not. I just wanted them out of my house.

Also if JJ was genuinely nice to people he might have had "real" friends to help him move out. JJ frequently stated, "No one likes a tool who uses them." This is true because not even you like this JJ. You said this ALL THE TIME and here you are behaving like a "tool." You are using another man for supply because he's available. At least you could have moved all your things out of the house since you had help but you left me to clean up your mess.

My family helped me clean while you abandoned everything. It took me 9 months to clean out the house. When I completely moved out on December 24th, 2021, I messaged Cece to inform her I left plastic storage containers on the curb. These were filled with your family heirlooms. The family portrait of your family and Mitch's books. It didn't feel right throwing them away so when I messaged her, she texted you and you ridiculed me. You treated it as trash and I like treasure. We are not the same. Plus, I had vacated the property and everything had to go to the curb but you know that because you didn't pay your taxes.

From here on out, I focused on myself. I've listed some ways I moved forward into healing:

- I worked on communication.
- Implemented boundaries
- Respected myself the way I expect others to.
- I kept in touch with my children until it was time to let go due to their lack of self-control and it was no longer safe for me to have a relationship with them.
- I slept a lot.
- I allowed my body to heal by exercising, listening to sleep meditations, taught myself coping skills to utilize during times of stress, became more aware of things that increased my stress, improved my diet and nutrition and spent time in nature.

- Went to the spa for deep tissue massages, facials, manicures, and pedicures.
- I took time off from work.
- I sold everything I owned to get the life I wanted.
- I listened to music.
- I took dance lessons. I learned how to Waltz, Salsa, Merengue, and Swing dance.
- I practiced forgiveness.
- I started journaling.
- I slowed down and learned to say "no" to others and "yes" to myself.
- I started painting and taking pictures again.
- Went to sporting events with friends.
- Took myself on "dates."
- Learned to cook and bake some of my favorite dishes.

9

BLESSING

Have you taken the time to consider that you were the blessing in someone's life?

Maybe the experiences you went through were to help you grow and not harm you.

Have you taken time to reflect on the positives that have come out of your situation?

I know this step can be painful, and it can also help you to move into your next chapter. In my experience, the storm comes right before it's time for you to move. It's time for you to become the person God specifically designed you to be. The storm is coming to test you and to see if you're ready for the next phase in your life. Will you pass the test, or will you collapse under pressure? Either way, you are in control of your choice. What will you choose?

Take a few minutes to answer these questions. Write down your answers on a piece of paper.

I'm serious. In order to move forward, you need to consider these things. If you skipped the section above, like I usually do, please go back and answer the questions.

Great, now we can move forward with the book!

Thinking about my personal situation, the storm of my marriage came to correct my path. When I met JJ, he seemed like the perfect guy. We hit it off right away. He was sweet, and things felt electric with him. I had never felt this way about anyone and thought he was the blessing my life was missing, but I was wrong. Haha, a woman admitting to the fact she was wrong. You can frame this page if you want, but it's true. I'll admit when I'm wrong, and I was wrong to think he was my blessing because he was the storm that came to correct my path.

I was his blessing. The way I see it, I was his last chance to change for the better. I was the Hail Mary play he'd been waiting on, the wild card sent to change his life but unfortunately, he failed to follow the playbook.

Think about it this way: In football, each coach has their own plays they've created in order to win the game. In marriage or any relationship, you need to strategize in order to win. God was our coach on the sidelines with the playbook in his hand. He carefully crafted each play, covering his mouth so the devil couldn't read his lips and would miss the play. You don't know why He sent a blessing into your ex's life. However, He knew what He was doing, and it wasn't for anyone else to know.

You were only to trust that God ordered your steps or called the play, and it's your job to follow through. He was waiting to see if you got to stay in and play the game His way, or if you were going to take control, call an audible, and mess up the play. God was watching to see if you really wanted what you prayed for, waiting to see if you were ready for the blessing He had prepared for you.

First, He needed to see if JJ was ready. JJ cried to his friends that no one was ever going to love him again while he puked into a trash can because he was so drunk. His friends, Ben and Emily, witnessed this firsthand at a bar. They told me how crushed he was when his ex-wife, Karen, left him. So, God sent me, and JJ called in an audible. He didn't want the blessing God sent to him, though.

I had expectations when I started dating JJ because I didn't want to be with a deadbeat dad. *SHOCKER* I actually didn't want to be a stepmom or date anyone who had been divorced. It wasn't something

I was originally open to, but the way I felt when I was around JJ was different than anyone I had dated before. Plus, the kids all had names I had picked out for my own kids as I grew up. I was JJ's blessing, and the children were mine for a bit.

Blessings upon blessings

You are the blessing. Your ex didn't see you were the blessing in front of them because they were blind. When someone is blind, they are limited in what they can see and feel because they are always looking past the moment. They can't live in the present and see what there is to see, constantly chasing ghosts that can't be caught. They can't see everything you are bringing to the table because they don't have the type of mindset to see it.

Most likely, you are dealing with someone who's been hurt as a child, and they are a result of their upbringing. Once upon a time, they might have been the golden child who was handed everything they wanted, and now they are being asked to earn what they want. Whatever it may be, they will never be happy with the expectations you've put in place because this is not how their world works. They can't reach your expectations because they choose not to and choose instead to fail. It's easier to run away than face reality. They don't want to help with anything because somewhere along the line, it means they're not perfect. You are threatening the very script they have written for their life, where they have to be perfect in every way. Ultimately, they are "gods" in their own lives and the only opinion that matters. This causes them to miss the blessings you are bringing into their lives.

Walk with me

Take a walk with me. Imagine you're a twenty-four-year-old woman who has entered into an exclusive relationship with a man who has three daughters. Life is going great until you get smacked upside your head, and you hear a voice that whispers, "He has a son with another woman." You're driving down the road and don't know what to do with this information. Well, that was twenty-four-year-old me. This is how I found out because my then-boyfriend was hiding his son, Xavier, with his previous girlfriend, Mia, from me. He dated Mia prior to his first marriage to Karen. I said nothing to him because I didn't want to sound crazy, but this was devastating.

A few weeks went by, and Cece, JJ's mother, brought the little boy, named Xavier, up. We were celebrating at JJ's sister Barb's house, and she was explaining the whole situation to me. I thought it was someone she was working with. My brain didn't grasp the whole conversation, as I didn't understand this was the son of the man I was dating. She then corrected me and said, "No, it's JJ's son. I take it he hasn't told you yet." My body reacted in an instant: heart pounding, shortness of breath, and the fictional walls around me were closing in. I stopped in my tracks at the news and had to remain calm as my daughters were playing a game of baseball in front of me on this hot, summer day in August. I was infuriated! How in the HELL did he keep this from me? Why did he keep his son from me? He told me he couldn't get women pregnant with a boy. Okay, JJ. Whatever.

I couldn't look at him for the rest of the night and couldn't stand being in the same room with him. I couldn't stand him! When we got home, I walked off my energy. I don't know if you're like me and you have to physically exert energy when you get mad, but it works for me. I walked for a long time that night.

I walked and walked until I couldn't walk any further. I loved someone who kept something that was vulnerable to him, or at least I thought it was because he was sensitive about it. Looking back, I now know he never wanted his son. This is a harsh reality for me to admit. It's so harsh I almost blew up in the middle of Steak-N-Shake when I figured this out when talking to Mia and Xavier.

It broke my heart! When I looked at my son's face, it could have killed me. Xavier is the most amazing human. He was brought into my life through extraordinary brokenness. This fact isn't lost on me. I looked at his face when he asked his mom to explain the complexity of his situation between his mom and dad to me. She looked at me and uttered the words, "JJ never wanted Xavier." A part of me died this day. How? Why? What? I couldn't think straight. The room was spinning. I had to go. I had to run. I had to get away. I didn't want to lose it in the middle of the restaurant, so I told my son to move. My chest tightened. My nerves kicked in. Adrenaline was pumping through my veins, as I wanted to punch something. I told him to get up from the table again. I had to get away, and he kept asking me, "Why?" I said "GET UP! I've got to go." His mom finally told him to get up and move.

I speed-walked to the bathroom and started naming five things I could see, touch, or feel to gain control of my anxiety. Of my ANGER! After a few minutes, I was calm and walked out of the women's bathroom returning to the table. I thought to myself, *What would cause someone to look at their child and disown them*? What monster does this? I thought I knew the man I had been married to for almost fourteen years. Why didn't I know this about him? How did I miss the signs? It was then that I realized the children were brought into my life for a reason. I was brought into their lives for a reason too. I didn't know what the blessing was, but I knew it was there.

God knew we needed each other. It doesn't matter how we came together because we have each other. In my eyes, and as others have told me, our kids wouldn't have had the opportunity to be a family with their dad and know him or each other if I wasn't around. I suppose this is a silver lining in all the brokenness we've experienced. I don't know how correct this is, but one's perspective is their own. I can't dispute it since it's not from my view. If I personally know you and you're reading this, please don't hold it against me if you have another perspective I haven't heard yet on this matter. I'm asking for your grace.

In these broken years, I was able to bless someone who can never repay me. I was sent to bless him, and he didn't see these blessings. Perhaps he was blinded by his ego. He thought he was the almighty in his mind. I guess I'll never know. What I do know is I stepped up to my cross and carried it. In the beginning, I didn't always do this with grace, but I learned grace through this storm.

I was a married, single wife raising children I didn't bring into this world, yet I chose to love them anyway. I didn't have to look over my shoulder to see if the script I wrote for my life was being followed. The cross said it all. He died for me, and I didn't understand it when this journey started but by the end of this relationship, my heart and soul were changed for eternity. The twenty-four-year-old woman I was, in the beginning, is dead. There are remnants of her, but she passed away as a stronger woman has emerged.

The blessings that were given to my ex-husband came in the form of me gladly spending time with our children, with no grumbling as some stepmothers do. I paid for one hundred percent of the bills for an extended time because he claimed not to have any money after he paid child support and his vehicle payment. I cleaned the house and took care of our multiple dogs with minimal help from him. I paid the emergency vet and car insurance bills because he refused to help me. I worked five jobs at one time to make ends meet because he refused to give me any money. I spent every waking hour slaving away, trying to provide for our family. In that time, I tried to be an understanding and supportive wife that helped her husband as he fought his addictions. I stayed when I should have left and gave him all the mercy and grace I could. I continued on this path until I couldn't anymore.

Change

One day, I woke up and decided something had to change. The blessings changed for him and shifted to me. I learned to love myself when he wouldn't love me. I loved myself when he wouldn't look at me. I was his wife, not a bank account or maid, supposed to be his forever love.

I was the woman he promised to love and cherish for all time until death do us part. In sickness and in health, he promised to love me no matter what. I felt sick. I felt helpless, empty, powerless, and trapped. I felt as though I was drowning no matter how hard I tried to swim. He was killing me, and I had enough.

Thankfully, I took my power back. I blessed myself. God gave me strength when I had none. He carried me into a season where I cut JJ off financially and emotionally. When we went to the grocery store, his allowance was $20 a week. This enraged JJ! He said, "I can't live off $20 of groceries a week." *Well, buddy, I had to, and so can you!* I thought to myself. I had to pay everything by myself without any help, and this is all I had left when the other bills were paid. If he didn't want to go back to the food bank, this was the best I could do. He either had to start helping or starve. JJ didn't like those options, so he started helping. He pretended to be happy about this, but I knew he wasn't. He was becoming snippy and short with me when we went to the store.

Getting JJ to take responsibility for the groceries was a huge accomplishment, I felt. I was happy with one less bill off my plate. Thank you, God! Success felt fantastic! I took this a step further to where I no longer allowed him to use my credit cards or agreed to finance unnecessary things like vehicles, campers, or frivolous items he requested, such as a massage gun. I was completely finished financing his irresponsibility.

Girl, it's time to invest in you

Yea, you read that right. I was maxed out financially, having used my credit cards to make ends meet when I didn't have enough money to make ends meet. I didn't care. I wanted to breathe so I started investing in myself. I didn't like where I was in life, so I started asking myself what needed to change for me to be happy. What needed to change for me to have a life that I really loved? Then I paid my credit card bills down, and I invested in personalized coaching. Yes! Your girl decided if I didn't have the skills to start something new, I would join every coaching class that made my heart dance. If it was a full-body hell yea, I was in. The more I engaged in these types of classes, the more my life changed.

I started to believe in my skills and abilities to do hard things, which brought me to a pivotal point in my life. I noticed people falling away from me and coming into my life. The ones I no longer needed left, while the ones I needed were brought into my life. This is the time I started my own health and wellness business, rising up and no longer needing JJ. He was no longer necessary in my life. God brought this business to me in the darkest moments of my life. The business held and carried me when I couldn't walk. These people who I now call family prayed over me, and this made all the difference.

God shined a light where I couldn't see. He showed me each blessing as I kept pushing forward. Keep going, friend. If it's not good, then it's not the end.

10

HINT OF GRAY

Mind your business: that's what my mother always said, except she always taught me to step up and help when needed. How would I know the difference?

Have you been there? You know you're supposed to step up and help but everyone is telling you to mind your business? I've been there, and this is how I ended up in a cold, loveless marriage. My friends and family minded their own business instead of helping me.

Don't fret, this turned out to be a good thing. I'm guessing you are probably thinking I'm pretty intense. LOL! I'm not crazy, but I'm someone who lives life on the edge of her seat. I no longer take days to make decisions. I just jump in! I make a decision and go for it.

Well, this brings me to the gray area of responsibility. After my ex-husband and I split for good, mountains started moving. I started praying that no one else would find themselves in the same position I found myself in.

Looking back, I had friends and non-blood family tell me they knew JJ was no good but didn't think it was their place to say anything to me. This infuriated me because I've always been the one to speak up when something was off.

In one instance, I was late going to class in high school and saw a couple spitting on each other. Yea, it's gross, but I noticed the boyfriend was blocking the girlfriend from leaving, and she was stuck in the stairwell where no one could see them. I spoiled his plans by trying to stop them, as he told me they were fine and told me to leave them alone. I told him I'd be on my way once he let her go and everyone could go to class. I never ran into them again. Not like this.

This is why I was angry when people started coming out of the woodwork when JJ and I split. I was being told he was no good, but no one stepped up to tell me about his past. No one told me he had robbed a bar he was working part-time at as a police officer or how he was kicked out of the Marine Corps boot camp because he skipped out on child support court. No one would warn me that I needed to get away from him. They knew this and watched me marry him anyway. Some friends and family I had.

It was in the first moments the first person came clean to me that I decided I was no longer going to keep quiet. I wasn't going to be a part of the silent majority and allow JJ to abuse someone else the way he did to me. I wasn't going to watch him tear someone else's life apart or let him target single mothers as he had done before. I wasn't going to allow him to create a brand-new circle of friends like he'd done in the past to escape his behavior. I wasn't going to allow it, so I stepped up to the plate and swung. No matter what happened, at least I tried.

I wasn't going to allow JJ to slink away and have zero consequences for everything he'd done. I decided it was my responsibility to pray for all the people he was going to be getting involved with. I prayed he wouldn't destroy their lives the way he did to mine and that they would see all his red flags. I prayed they would ask him deep questions, exposing his intentions and causing him to flee. He especially didn't like the questions asking where the kids were or about their moms.

How do I know?

I know because the women he cheated on me with during our marriage and the woman he has dated since our divorce have done background checks on him. They know about me and used social media to contact me. They wanted to know about the moms of my children and how I ended up in this mess I call life, so I told them everything that was important for them to know. They have even asked me why my ex and I didn't divorce sooner. According to them, he couldn't divorce me because "he owed the IRS $7,000.00 in back taxes and wasn't allowed to divorce me until it was paid," but he owed over $65,000.00 and he wasn't in the process of divorcing me. JJ faked a text message conversation on his phone through Instagram with "me." He then screenshotted the conversation and sent it to his affair partner "proving we were in the divorce process." She then messaged me and sent me the photo of the fabricated conversation to show me proof. She also messaged me stating *"And all I wanted to do was explain that I just figured it out. I don't want to be the other woman and wanted you to know he was lying to you too. You don't need to respond. Be well."* She sent this message to me on March 25, 2021 at 12:18 in the morning. Oh, the stuff I learned when these women contacted me. Who in the HELL was I married to? I had no freaking idea! Actually, I did; I was married to a monster.

I helped these women get away from JJ. I know some of you may not want to help the next person because you got away and you're staying far away from it all. You don't want to get mixed up in the next mess but the way I see it, I have a responsibility to help this new person. I want to help them the way no one would help me. Just because my life was blown up doesn't mean this person should be abused and taken advantage of by JJ. I'm the wild card. I'm not scared to tell the truth.

I've always worn my heart on my sleeve but right next to it is my shield. It's the armor I wear when I'm riding up next to someone, a person I fully intend to help. I'm not backing down, and you shouldn't either. It's my responsibility to help this next person, even if there are shades of gray. I'm not going to walk away when I know they need help and I can help, so I'm going to pick up my sword and go to battle. I'm strong, faithful, and fearless when defending others.

Though I may be small, I'm mighty. I'm not scared of my past but more concerned about what will happen to these people if I don't speak up. Interestingly enough, it's not only women my ex-husband uses. I told you I'm calling it how I see it, and he uses men too. I've watched him, using men he can get attention from. I just don't know how far he takes it with them. I do know he will use them to get attention, joining sports teams or going to a bar just to have someone's attention. He will get them to help him move from place to place or serve them a scripted story to gain a "friend" to feel sorry for him. I call these flying monkeys.

These are the people he "feeds" sob stories to in order to get them to feel sorry for him. He uses this to manipulate them, turning them against me and using them to gather information or "spy" on me in order to help him. They are individuals who will carry out his further abuse without him being present.

I know this because the police officer friend he brought into my home was a jerk. It felt like JJ told him to behave this way because he knew it would cause harm to me. This was his "flying monkey" in action. The way the officer behaved towards me created an unsafe environment and I knew by the way he was carrying himself he believed the stories he had been told. Before JJ came over he mentioned the officer was used to "hostile" environments so why did he create one in my house? He knew better and did it anyway. In my opinion, he was trying to intimidate and scare me.

He's the new supply. The supply does everything to keep their manipulator happy and this is what I observed. The supply moved according to JJ's details. I knew this because he was fighting me every step of the way. JJ was also living with him and his wife on their futon in the basement. It was a weird reality for me. I guess my ex would literally use anyone and everything he could to live the life he'd scripted for himself.

Moving forward, responsibility has often been gray in this

chapter of life, but I've chosen to embrace it. Embracing the problem has led me to see past the destruction, and I looked over its shoulder as I embraced the challenge to see what is on the horizon.

Can you see it? Close your eyes for a moment and see how your life could change when you stop and breathe.

Imagine what your life could look like.

Who will you help on your journey?

Who are you going to take along with you?

Pause for a moment and write this down.

I'm taking you with me. Will you join me?

This way, we can work together to help those who need us.

BIG CHANGES

11

REBUILDING ME

In the cool, fall months of late 2019, I started a new love affair. It's a love I've found to be unending and built on a renewed foundation that was once crumbling. This love affair is one I decided would be with myself.

I know, I was raised in a time when focusing on yourself was viewed as selfish and egotistical; however, in my opinion, society got this massively wrong. Hear me out, friend. My first teachers were my parents, and I thank them for doing everything they could to raise my siblings and me properly. I know they did everything they could to give us the best life they could.

But I watched my parents work themselves to the bone and never saw them take time to care for themselves. I'm not talking about a night out with friends or family. I'm talking about that real type of kindness you give yourself. The type of kindness you give the person you are madly in love with. I never saw either of my parents give themselves this kind of self-love.

This is the type of love every one of us deserves and should have no matter what. I'm not saying we need to get engaged and marry to receive this type of love. We need to stop looking for others to validate and love us because we were created for love. A love we should be taught growing up, and if you didn't learn this type of love growing up, then you can learn how to do it now.

I'm thirty-nine years old, and I have had to teach myself this kind of love. I wanted this type of love. I craved this type of love. I tried for years to get this type of love from someone who refused to love me back, even though he promised in front of God and our families that he would. But he didn't, and he never will. He's too broken to love anyone and can't even love himself, so I stopped asking him to give me what he wasn't capable of giving me. I finally saw JJ for the man he is. I took the gold lacquer in my cup and poured it into my cracks. This allowed me to hold the pieces that have broken away, heal them and fit them back together being more beautiful than before. As I've healed, I realized my hurts are beautiful because they've pushed me to be a better person.

In Ecclesiastes 7:3, it reads, "Sorrow is better than laughter, for by the sadness of the face the heart becomes better" (Ecclesiastes 7:3, The Scriptures. Institute for Scripture Research). This verse has become my mantra for healing. I've come to realize every test I've encountered being with JJ wasn't to hurt me. He came into my life to expose the deep-rooted hurt within me, the hurt I didn't realize was there. Ultimately, Satan sent him to destroy me. He wanted me shattered beyond all repair, but I know my God. I know my heavenly Father wouldn't allow this to pass through His hands. He used Satan's evil plan for good and redirected this plan to help me reconnect with the little girl I've long since forgotten.

This little girl God needed me to remember, He needed her to come alongside me as my deepest hurts were exposed. My husband purposefully refused to love me and walked away from me on a daily basis. He spent his time showboating as a wonderful man on social media to gain attention but stonewalled his wife when she desperately wanted to give and receive affection. This behavior triggered my abandonment issues, and he knew this. He did this in an attempt to control me and would punish me for weeks by not talking to me. He knew this was psychological warfare and was happy using it.

I know this seems harsh but his manipulation was specific and calculated. JJ punished me so he could force me to comply with his demands. Day in and day out, he kept exposing me to the same conversation in a variety of exposures. Anyone in sales knows the way to eventually get someone to buy their product is to expose, involve, and upgrade. This is exactly what I was exposed to over and over again, except I never complied.

Yes, you read that right. I never complied with the abuse JJ did. I started investing in myself by listening to business coaches who taught me how to increase my purpose as a person, eliminate debt, how to manifest what I wanted out of life, how to live outside of the validation of others, and how to live out my passions by helping others. When I hired these coaches, I started planting an orchard within myself. Instead of spending all that I was making, I started honoring myself and God by growing myself. He put me here for a reason, and these coaches were hired to help me figure this out. While my husband was focused on tearing me down and belittling me so he could use me in the worst way, I was busy creating a new life my family would truly enjoy. I was determined to build my legacy and empire with or without my husband standing by my side.

In this season, I chose to become the best version of myself. I launched my own health and wellness business, started helping those in poverty, and focused my efforts on what I could change in my life.

Now, I'm guessing you already know this made JJ irate, and it did. Since I never signed the finance papers for the four-door Jeep or the teardrop camper he wanted, his affair partner started questioning him. This is the worst thing that can happen to a narcissist because you are challenging the false reality they have so carefully crafted for someone else.

The two of us, together, destroyed the scripted world he had created. He loved cutting out of work early and heading up to Whatchamacallit, Wisconsin, every other weekend after he got paid to see Kacey. I hoped he was getting help from a friend for his mental health as he said, but I knew better. I had confronted him about cheating on me in July 2020, and it was now March 2021. He swore he wasn't cheating on me because he said, "I barely have enough for one woman, let alone two." We were not intimate and his behavior was indicating otherwise.

Whenever JJ was around me, and he used this tactic, he wore a smug smile on his face. He thought he was going to get whatever he planned. He had Satan sitting on his shoulder, controlling his every move, but he underestimated my trust in God. While JJ was attempting to punish me, God used these silent moments as a training ground.

In these moments, God would speak to me. He would put thoughts and ideas in my head before they ever came to me in real time. I was made aware of things before they happened and eventually started asking God what was going on or what was I missing. He would tell me, or I asked Him to bring someone into my situation to tell me. This is how much of the information I was seeking, regarding the situation with JJ, came to me. The more I trusted in God, the more He started showing me things I needed to see. He had to know I was truly open to His wisdom.

This is where I found freedom.

12

CAUGHT IN THE CROSSFIRE

Watching the husband you love walk out of the life you've built is hard, but watching your parent walk away from your home is much harder. Being a child is a challenge on its own, but knowing how to connect with your hurting parent brings a new level of hard. It's a level a child should never be asked to connect with them on. I know because my parents separated and divorced when I was in high school. They didn't put me in the middle, but somehow I ended up there. They didn't ask me to, but that's where I landed. I didn't belong in the middle, yet so many children of divorced parents find themselves there. I'm here to help them get out. It's time our children have voices.

Before we deep-dive into this chapter, I'm going to ask for grace. Some of you might be parents and some not. I would still encourage you to read this chapter. It may even help you heal your inner child issues if you were a child of divorce. You may find some of the information helpful to someone you know.

I also am sharing information from my own life as a teen of divorce and as a trauma survivor who has children who have gone through a divorce. My children have also survived multiple divorces and deserve to be heard. I want to give children a voice it seems as though they never have. I'm tired of hearing children are resilient and will push through it. In my opinion, this is the wrong approach when handling divorce. We need to help children process the pain and grow through it. We can be better so as to not allow our children to be caught in the crossfire.

Setting the stage

As children grow up, they are allowed to be children, or they are taught to be little adults. I've experienced this through my own life and marriage. As a child, I didn't have many adults around me who were emotionally available, so I learned to cope in my own way. I thought I had to be a perfectionist for people to love me. I sought attention by being perfect or fighting to be heard. Please don't get me wrong; my parents showed me love and affection but, on some level, it wasn't the correct connection for me. Parents can only connect on the level they know of. They can do their best to love you, and it still won't be enough.

Each of us is a different person, which is why we are uniquely our own. This is why it's important to dig deep within ourselves and get to know who we truly are. This approach is something I've been working on for the last two years. It's hard work looking in the mirror, but in the end, it will all be worth it. I'd rather get to know myself than not have a clue about who I am. This is it, friend; we are living life now. You have to decide if you like life or if you want something else.

This is the same place our children are in. When they're standing in the crossfire, they are asking themselves if they like life or if they like where this is going. They are wondering where they need to step up or "land" to help Mom or Dad in the separation and divorce stage of life. They are taking on responsibilities that are not theirs to handle. If they're young adults like I was, they're trying to figure this out mostly on their own, and your job is to help them land on solid ground.

Solid ground

I know from experience solid ground may not seem feasible, but it is. They need solid ground to land on so they can have stability. As an adult, it's best to remain as calm as possible and weigh your options. I'm not going to list them here because I don't know what you are up against in your life.

In my situation as a teen, my mom kept the house and gave my siblings and me stable ground; however, when it came to my own divorce, I chose to sell everything I had to get out from the mountains of debt to survive. I could have fought the IRS and stayed in my house, but I would have struggled. I would have been keeping a house and stuff that kept me trapped in an awful situation and wouldn't have been able to pay off my ex-husband's taxes he refused to pay. This gave me a leg up in life. I could pay off what I could while leaving my attorney to deal with my ex-husband.

Did it hurt letting those things go? Yes, it did. Knowing I had to sell the house I watched my babies grow up in sucked. No mom wants to let go of the home she raised her babies in, but I had to make the best decision I could for my family. I texted my kids and included them in my decisions. I gave them the voice I often felt they weren't allowed to have. I asked what they would like to keep from the house, and they told me, which made me feel better when I went through their belongings.

It was hell packing up my children's rooms, and if you witnessed this, you would have thought I was packing up rooms from children who had passed away because this is how it felt. Letting go of this house meant my kids would never again grace its halls nor would they wake up, walk down the hall, and give me morning snuggles or goodnight kisses. It would all be gone. I had to grieve the past to let myself let go. It was complicated because my feelings were attached to the outcome, but it's alright for you to grieve. It's alright for you to give your kids a voice. It's alright to mourn, just make sure you do it in a way that's healthy for you and them. Finally, make sure to detach from the situation because the situation doesn't dictate who you are as a person. It was an experience in your life, not a definition of who you are.

Separated

This chapter of life isn't my favorite. As a teenager, watching a parent move out of our family house is hard. I found myself documenting what was taking place while my mom was working. I took pictures of what my dad was moving out of the house. I felt like a double agent. In my own way, I was trying to make sure everyone was happy when no one was.

I made sure I didn't repeat this same situation when going through my divorce. Actually, my twin daughters were living with their mom, and my son was living with his stepdad. They were in two different households, and Mara was living on her own. I'm so proud of her! She told me her plans long ago. She's doing an amazing job living life on her terms. I'm so proud of the wonderful young woman she's turning out to be. I had to share my proud mom moment in all of this chaos.

My ex-husband and I separated in March 2021, and he refused to tell our children. Telling my children was the hardest part of the separation for me. It was one thing for him to move out and lie about his double life, but it was another thing for him to show up to track meets as he stood by me, pretending as though nothing was going on. What was worse was when he stood with me, having conversations with the kids, and he refused to tell them we were separated. He had the audacity to cheat on me but wouldn't tell our kids we were getting a divorce. What a coward!

He did, however, tell them he took the dogs on a camping trip and that I was "mad" because he took the dogs. Nope, I'd never be mad because he took our dogs on a trip. I'd be happy because they got to go on an adventure. It's our job to give our fur babies their best life. Fortunately, he told our son, Xavier, this untruth, and Xavier called his bluff. He knew right away something was wrong and messaged me. I've always been honest with my kids, and I've told them if they want to know the truth to ask me, so Xavier asked me what was going on.

This was the moment I had been dreading. I gave JJ two months to come clean with our kids, but he kept saying he had to find the "right" time. HELLO, there is no right time when you're about to blow your kids' lives up. Just saying! Out with it already!

Again, all the responsibility fell on my shoulders like it always did. I was the one who told the kids we were separated because their dad had an affair. I also cautioned them that their dad was drinking and driving. I told them not to get in the car with him, as it wasn't safe for them to be in the car with him as he had prior accidents I later discovered. He has a public record noting criminal misde-meanors for operating a vehicle while intoxicated; endangering another person while failing to stop after the accident; causing damage to their attended vehicle in 2009 and then crashing into another vehicle in 2011; failing to stop while intoxicated; damaging an unattended vehicle. This didn't include the time he smashed through our fence in the front yard. He backed up and barely missed our house. I couldn't stand the thought that my kids' lives would be at risk of getting into the car with him, so I told them this. I wasn't going to risk their lives to protect his drunkenness anymore. I can't believe he has two hit and runs on his record and still has a driver's license. What were the police officers thinking? He should have been in jail for these, in my opinion. God, I hope he never kills anyone because he chooses to drink over getting sober. It makes me sick thinking about it.

When informing my children of our divorce, that was one of the worst moments of my life. It was telling my kids something so personal my ex wouldn't even be honest about after he made the choices he did. Cece, my ex-mother-in-law acted like I was awful for telling them when JJ was micromanaging me at track meets to keep me quiet. When I asked him if he was sorry about the affair, JJ mustered up an expression that made him appear sorry, but he wasn't. I've witnessed enough of his facial expressions to know the truth. He didn't care one bit that he had hurt me. He didn't even care about our family. The only person JJ cared about was himself, focused on his next "fix," and that's all he's ever cared about.

And the kicker was Xavier asked me about this situation when I was off work. I didn't realize it was in our family Snapchat app. When I answered him, my kids were at school. I was glad they knew the truth, but I was mortified they found out at school. I couldn't even imagine what was going through their minds. Then I started getting texts from the girl's mother, Karen, that read, *"I don't know how the girls know but they found out somehow."* I quickly messaged Karen back and let her know the text had come from me.

The girls must have messaged my ex because he started texting Karen. She hadn't heard from him in over a year and a half. We figured this would happen; he was trying to save his own skin. She said, *"Surprise, surprise, look who's texting now."* We knew he was going to try and blame me, which he did, but thankfully I had told everyone the truth before he started doing damage control for himself. The things he cooked up were actually truths about himself, but it was easier to blame me than take responsibility for his actions. Go ahead and blame me, babe; you can't hide from the truth forever.

Stay

They say the truth shall set you free, and I'm glad it did in my case. My children seemed to have more respect for me since I told them the truth, no matter how painful it was. I listened to them about the divorce and they surprised me. They listened to me. Remember, I've been in the mom role since they were three and five years of age. I told them I loved them, and I didn't want to lose them.

The next thing I knew, all my children invited me to remain in their lives. I was shocked! I knew they loved me but in the back of my mind, I had hoped it wasn't only because I was married to their dad. It's kind of like the little girl in me was nervous she was going to be left again. Not this time. I have worked so hard on my relationships with my kids that they invited me to stay. I don't know if you're a stepparent but, to me, this was worth more than gold. Having these children in my life was everything I had prayed for, and they still chose me. God does work miracles, and this is one. He put me exactly where I needed to be, with them.

If Rocky had a daughter, that would be me

Every year, I relish watching my kids participate in sports. I love seeing my girls, Piper and Zoe, as cheerleaders cheering Xavier on during football season. Watching Piper fly through the air always excites me. It blows my mind how graceful she is when she flies through the air. To be completely transparent, I feel relieved every time her cheerleading base catches her. I take a deep breath and think, *Thank you, God! She did amazing, and thank you for keeping her safe.* Then there's Zoe who does crazy backflips. I don't know how she flips so quickly but she does them so fast, I can barely keep up with her. Then during the spring, Piper manages the track team while Zoe and Xavier compete in the long jump and other running events. Seeing them is the height of my day.

Although, before I go to these events, I have to prepare myself. I have to prepare to see my ex-spouse, who mentally tortured me and then conditioned me to pretend as though everything was alright. At first, he walked around with his arms postured to convey this is his territory. As he paced the fence during football season, but as the season persisted, he dropped them. He stopped walking around, trying to intimidate people; maybe he was trying to intimidate me. I didn't care what he was doing, since I already made up my mind about him.

Before each sporting event, I decided who was calling the shots, and that was me. I wasn't going to back down to my abuser. He could walk, stand, or breathe by me, but I wasn't going to leave. I was there to support my kids, as this time was the most precious gift I had. He already robbed me of my chance of getting to see Mara participate in show choir, so I'd be danged if I lost this time too. I had to be tough like Rocky! I had to look fear in the face and let it know I wasn't scared. I'm living on my terms, not yours.

This mindset served me well, and it can help you too. It would be a great servant to your children to teach them to look fear in the face and knock it out. Fear is only as powerful as we allow it to be. When you make a decision and pursue it, you are no longer thinking about it but acting. Once you act on your decision, there is no longer space for fear. In my case, JJ, who I was supposed to fear, stopped following me around at these sporting events. He stopped trying to control me and left me alone, and I was no longer scared of him or anyone for that matter. He lost his power over me.

I focused where I needed to, and then he stopped coming to sporting events for a while. He didn't show up to football games, which that will be on him. He cashed in his quality time with our son for other things. As for me, you can find me on the sidelines cheering my kids on, unless I'm sick. You can rise again just like I am. You have the power, my friend; it's time to punch fear in the face, and here are some tips to help you on your way.

Tips to help your kids in the crossfire of divorce or marital conflict

1. Remind your children you love them. There is nothing more important during this time than reminding your children that you love them. It's okay to have your up and down days, but remember to still express love to them as best you can.
2. Allow your children to be children. During this time, your children need the freedom to be angry or sad in this time. They are losing a family they have grown accustomed to being with, no matter how bad the situation is. There's a chance they taught themselves to focus on the positive, as this was a way they learned to survive.
3. Never put them in the middle. I know it might be tempting to buy your child a cell phone and create rules that the other parent can't take it away. This will only cause your

child more problems, and I'm sure this isn't what you want for them. It also isn't a good idea to use this phone as a weapon. Their job is not to be a little parent while they are in the other household, and if you expect them to be a parent, I would encourage you to reevaluate your parenting methods. I know we want to protect our children, but this approach is more likely to cause damage and rob your child of a childhood. Fight for their childhood and keep them out of the middle.

4. If you treat your child like a little spouse, STOP. Your child is a child. It's not their job to be your micro-spouse. It's not your daughter's job to raise her siblings, chase them through the grocery store when you can't control them, or refuse to call the other parent because you don't want to update them appropriately. It also isn't your son's job to be the "man of the house," when your ex-husband moves out. Don't put this responsibility on him; it's not his job to bring in the money you're losing when he leaves. I know it's hard, but you can figure it out; it's your job. The kids don't want to be your micro-spouse. If you want a spouse, go date someone but please don't put this responsibility on your child.

5. Be the adult. Handle the lawyer, court, and bills without involving your child. They don't need to know why you went to court. They need to focus on being a kid. Soothe and relax them.

6. Allow them to love the other parent. They will eventually figure things out on their own. If you pressure them into believing your views about the other parent, it will take your child longer to learn the truth. Also, let them love anyone who's good for them and comes into their lives. More people loving them isn't bad, and it could actually help them learn what healthy relationships look like. It's a training ground for the future. I wish I would have been allowed to think for myself growing up.

7. Keep supporting your children no matter how hard it is. They need you and may show you that need in the most unloving ways. This is a hard key to remember. During this time, your kids might push you away, and that's okay. They are learning how to cope with the separation/divorce. Just make sure you are there when they're ready to talk. Teach them they can trust adults, even when life gets hard.

Most of all, keep going. Raising children, overcoming trauma, and divorcing all at the same time is crazy hard. You are worth it! You are amazing! You can do this, keep going!

13

CAUGHT NAKED

Have you ever walked around naked, in public?

No? I dare you to.

Yes, that's right. I dare you to get naked and honest with yourself.

So many people walk around naked but don't realize it.

Take Adam and Eve, for instance. They were walking around in the garden, happy as could be, except they didn't acknowledge the fact they were naked.

They let it all hang out.

Breast, butt, penis, scrotum ... It all hung out.

They were raw and authentic. Well, until they bit into an apple. An apple they weren't supposed to touch. An apple they were given to cause exposure. An apple causes everlasting effects on them.

This apple is like the reality we hide from and is not far from what real people hide from. Some people don't know it's there while others hide from it. Kinda like trying to tell people about being abused and violated and losing your innocence, but they don't want to acknowledge it. They would rather sweep it under a rug and only care about how they feel. They would prefer to pretend you were never assaulted by the person you loved most.

Rip the rug out from underneath them

That's right, expose all the gory details and rip the rug out from underneath them.

This is how I think Adam lived until he bit into the apple. He was living happily until he bit into the apple. When he bit into the apple, everything was exposed. All of a sudden, he wondered why he was walking around a garden with his junk hanging out. He wondered if Eve was looking at him with eyes of perversion. Sizing up his package and wondering if there was another man out there with a larger package who could satisfy all her wants and needs more than he could. Would this man dive deep within her, giving a pleasure she never felt? Would she care about Adam, even though she was created from his rib, or would she run away with another man?

Eve could see everything Adam embodied, but she wanted more pleasure. Her mouth salivated with greed. She saw everything around her that she wanted control over, and she was willing to go against the sacred rules in the garden to get what she wanted. This is what it was like living with my abuser. I'm guessing this is what it was like living with your abuser too. They won't stop diving deep until they have everything they want, and then it still won't be good enough.

I'll do what I must, to get what I want

You may not have thought about it, but Eve was lusting after what she couldn't have; that's why she got Adam to bite into the fruit. She wanted to be as powerful as God, but there was no way she could prepare for it. God had already written their endings before He wrote their beginnings. He knew this would happen. He knew the screen would fall from Adam's eyes as he chewed the sweet, supple apple, when the juice dripped off his lips. He knew Adam would no longer look at Eve the same.

Adam had pure eyes living for the good of God and the garden, but Eve was lustful after the things in this world. She wanted what wasn't hers without earning it. What God had given her wasn't good enough. She had to have more, and she wouldn't stop until she had what she wanted according to her will.

Eve analyzed everything in the garden. She didn't stop to consider what she had was good. She didn't stop to consider what she had was provided for her without any labor of her own. She didn't stop to consider that God gave her a husband who loved her and wasn't leaving the garden every other weekend to have an affair with a woman the next town over. She didn't consider it because she was self-absorbed.

We could say Eve was curious; however, this would be an understatement. She was greedy and vengeful. She didn't care that her actions would hurt the person she was married to. Eve was going to go above and beyond to become all-powerful, so she took the apple and gave it to her spouse. She made herself out to be a loving wife but instead, she was like a narcissist waiting for her prey to take the bait. The bait she provided so she could see what would happen. She didn't have the guts to be the woman she wanted to be, so she preyed on the beautiful gift God gave her and DESTROYED it.

She didn't destroy it only for herself but for the rest of her lifetime. Eve decimated it so badly that her legacy was nothing but crumbs left on the ground for other abusers to pick up.

She was the one who opened doors for evil to enter this world. She stepped on those around her to get what she wanted, framing it in a way that looked "okay" to society. Every abuser who has come after her has gotten more skilled at deceit because it was planted by her in her actions, taking root from a seed she planted. The only fruit you will encounter from this seed will have death written on it.

The fruit of death

This is what my life was like behind closed doors. I was plagued with years of negativity and thinking because of the way I had grown up. My parents did the best they could but no matter what, a person will have trials in their life. My parents tried to encourage me and tell me I could be anything I wanted to be when I grew up, but it didn't help.

For whatever reason, I thought negatively about myself, and I got it in my head that I needed to earn the love I was given. God doesn't promise we will never have hard times. He does promise us that He will be with us through it all, though.

Growing up, somewhere along the line I got it in my head I had to be perfect. I had to be the perfect person and turn the other cheek, no matter what. The only people I stood up to were my siblings in the typical rivalries siblings have until I got into elementary school. The kids in elementary school were mean. They didn't understand what a learning disability was, so they shamed me for having one. They thought they could catch my learning issues and treated me as an outcast. The only people who would carry on a conversation with me were my teachers.

My teachers were nice to me. They didn't judge me, and it was from them I grew stronger. These were the people who taught me what life was about outside of my parents. My teachers even allowed me to stand up for myself when my classmates were bullying me.

The bullying had gotten so bad that by sixth grade, I stood up to a kid on the playground. I don't remember what he said to me, but he was bullying my sibling, a friend of ours and me. It got so bad that I put the kid in a headlock and when he was trying to get away from me, he ended up causing us to slam into the garage door toward the back of the school property. I wasn't necessarily proud to scrap in the school yard, but I had to. I had to fight my classmates to get them to stop hurting me and those I cared about.

Behind closed doors

This is what it was like for me when no one else was around. I had to fight to keep myself protected and alive, pretending as though I didn't know what was going on, even if I did. I analyzed my living situation and decided the best action to take.

This caused others around me to think I didn't know what was going on. At some points early on in my relationship with JJ, I didn't know what was going on. I'm not ashamed to admit it. Why, you might be wondering? I don't feel ashamed because I didn't know this kind of evil existed in the world.

That's right; I knew there was evil, but I didn't realize it could come in the form of my ex or in the ex's exes. Before I got into this relationship, I didn't know that evil physically walked the planet. I thought it was something the Bible talked about and referenced so we would behave.

So, yes, I'm not ashamed because I didn't know. I didn't know there were people in the world who would choose to attach themselves to a personality disorder rather than deal with reality. I didn't know there were people who would pretend to have a true, genuine heart to create a facade for themselves to manipulate others to like them.

Anyone who thinks poorly of someone in my position who has been abused in a relationship and who didn't know what was happening to them should look in the mirror and ask themselves how they came to this conclusion. If you're so quick to judge, I'd challenge you to think about the circumstances.

Ask yourself these questions:

Were you there every time something happened?

Did you take the time to help this person get out of the situation?

Did you know what was going on but didn't have the audacity to say anything?

Did you find the situation funny and tout yourself to be smarter than the abused person?

Did you put the abused person down?

Did you create an environment or relationship where this person could come to you for help?

Were you a part of the problem?

Have you apologized for your role in the situation?

Have you said you would first support them and then, later on, belittle them for speaking up about the abuse?

Did you have their back when they tried to get away from the abuse, or did you make it worse?

Did you make them feel like they had nowhere to turn?

Did you abuse them too?

Did you know the abuser was lying to the victim but said nothing to help?

Why didn't you help them?

Not ashamed

I don't feel ashamed because I didn't know better. I didn't know the person I loved with all my heart was intentionally abusing me. I didn't know he would be nice to me, then mean to me, then nice again to create a trauma bond to confuse my brain. I didn't know he would do this to create a trauma bond within the physiological parts of my body to make it to where I was so confused, I didn't know what to do.

If you want to shame someone for not knowing what was going on when they were being abused, then you are just as guilty of abuse as the abuser. I say this because I've recognized what the process of trauma-bonding looks like, and since I've gotten away from my abuser, I've realized other people in my extended family have attempted to get me trauma-bonded to them.

The people who have judged me for how I handled things behind closed doors when I wasn't supported, and I was having to fight to keep myself safe from someone who was rigid and vile, tried to put me in bondage too.

It broke my heart that this is what happened to me and maybe you too. It breaks my heart that there are so many evil people willing to take advantage of the good people that are in this world. What doesn't break my heart is the fact I GOT OUT. God drove my abuser out of my house, and while God was working on my heart, teaching me how to get away, I learned how to overcome the abuse while God carried me.

He carried me through Egypt, away from the abuse and into the wilderness. He placed me a safe distance away from my abuser so I could truly learn how to be the person He needed me to be.

Goodbye Egypt, Hello Wilderness

At the moment God drove evil out of my home, I was floored at the power He has. I could tell by looking at JJ he had to flee from our home. He couldn't stand what was going on.

It was like good and evil were battling it out in my family room. That's when I had a moment just like Adam did when he bit into the apple. I experienced this same moment in July 2020 when I asked God to show me what I wasn't seeing. I asked Him to show me what was going on because I knew in my gut, I was overlooking something. And God did. He showed me who I was really with. He exposed every detail, and it frightened me.

This moment has been burned into my brain so well that I stopped when I was still talking to God, and I quietly asked, "Who the BLEEP am I married to?" At that moment, God picked me up and carried me. That was the moment He became my everything, the moment I started checking in with God before I made any moves.

I felt safer with God. He made it to where I could stay in my house until I was ready to leave and sell it. I felt God place a sacred space around me that JJ wouldn't enter, and he never did.

Egypt has fallen

When JJ walked into the house after his affair partner contacted me he blew by me. I tried calling him, and he told me he was on the way home. It was a Thursday, and I was on spring break. His affair partner had done a background check on him to see if he was married, flying into Indianapolis from Wisconsin to see where he lived. He told her some garbage story about how he couldn't take her into the house because it was being fumigated.

I think this part of his lie is hilarious because the house wasn't covered. I was also still at home, seeing as I was the one paying the mortgage and he was just a man-child playing in a fantasy land he worked diligently to create. I, on the other hand, was relaxing at home, waiting for Egypt to fall. I had already asked God to encourage someone to tell me the whole truth. I knew there was someone out there; I just had to wait.

Waiting

Patiently waiting was hard for me. I wanted to know the truth, but I also didn't want my life to fall apart. Waiting was worth it because this time God changed my heart. I wasn't the most patient person in my twenties. Actually, I was the backside of a donkey if you wanted to know the truth, just like many twenty-something-year-olds are. We have to learn through life experiences to gain a wider view of the world. This time, I gained the experience I prayed for.

It was January 2020 when JJ's affair partner flew into the city. He came home that night and told me "the guys" had changed plans without talking to him first. I thought it was weird and nice at the same time. I appreciated getting to spend a little extra time with him, but I also learned that he paid for her to be put up in a hotel when he wouldn't even take me on a date. He blatantly refused to go on a date with me even if I paid for it. I was the man and woman in the relationship so why shouldn't I be paying? But he threw a temper tantrum saying how he hated going out. He just wanted to stay at home, so it was weird he put so much energy into the multiple affair dates.

Multiple affair dates, you ask? Yes, I know he had these because I paid close attention to the locations he told me was visiting compared to what his affair partner told me. He would also drive through toll booths and the cameras would snap a picture of his license plate. The bills would later come to me for payment, since his Jeep was in my name. I had proof of what states he was going to instead of being with me.

This is how his affair partner and I met. She messaged me through Messenger asking if JJ was my husband. Then she attached a screenshot of a message he had sent her. He fabricated a story about how we were separated and living in separate rooms in our house when the kids were there, but I would live at my mother's house during the weeks the kids were not there.

We had a long conversation about this because he was lying out of his backside. I informed her that we in fact slept in the same bed, were still sexually active with each other, and he nor I slept in other rooms. This shocked her. I went on to answer her questions about who did the laundry and cooked his food. I'll never forget our conversation. The look on her face, as she explained everything to me, was that of one being mortified. She couldn't believe what he did to me and to her. Plus, just like me, she thought she had found the "one."

JJ is a smooth liar and a con man at that. He will use anyone and anything to get ahead in life, so we, ladies, did the next best thing as he rushed into the house away from my presence. He huddled in the kitchen as Kasey and I confronted him, together, as she was on Face-Time with me.

We asked him if he was *"ready to man up and have a conversation."* A conversation he lied about saying he had already had with me. In a conversation, he told her that he wanted a divorce multiple times, but he just didn't go through with it because he still owed tax money to the IRS, and he couldn't get divorced until it was all paid off. That's laughable because the only person who ever mentioned divorce was me.

I mentioned it because he was drunk all the time and when he didn't have a drink, he would have seizures because his body couldn't function without alcohol. The doctors told him to stop drinking on three separate trips to the emergency room because he was at risk of developing pancreatitis, but he kept drinking.

After the trips to the emergency room, I was the one who got blamed for his drinking because "I loved him too much." I don't know about you but if you have a good woman, hold on to her because only a drunken idiot would let one go, especially if his first real affair partner was Jameson Irish Whiskey, and that's the truth. Why would you want to be with a good woman when you can sit at home and get drunk all the time?

I'll never understand why someone would choose addiction over their family but that's not for me to figure out. I loved JJ where he was at, and I was still made out to be the bad guy.

Driven

JJ and I sat down in the family room to talk about the affair. I wanted answers, and it was in this moment I felt like what I thought Adam would have felt like when he bit into the apple. I saw everything for what it was. I saw JJ as the snake he was. His pupils were expanded so wide, his entire eyes were black. The white on the sides of his eyes were gone. Looking at him was so creepy.

I asked him why he cheated on me, and his response was *"I was done. I'm depressed. I'm over it."* These are the most pathetic words I've ever heard anyone speak. He was done because I was no longer putting up with the abuse or his lack of support.

He didn't like that I was holding him accountable, and he didn't want to live up to the duties he swore by when we got married. I took our vows seriously, but to him, they were just something to say. They were nothing but a game to him.

JJ didn't have much to say for himself. The conversation was short, and he admitted that he was a coward. I'm not going to argue with that. Cowards use their kids to get married and secure a life with someone they only want until the other person expects an actual husband or wife. JJ would move on to other single moms trying to get them to fall in "love" with him. The sad part is he is actually not capable of loving anyone but himself and can't see beyond his pain. He could never be the husband I needed him to be, and he would never be the father my kids needed him to be.

He will never be the man he was brought here to be. It's sad and true. I'm thankful that Kasey contacted me and used her voice to make both of our lives better. I wasn't going to be a wife who followed her husband around snooping to make sure he was being faithful. That was a waste of my time. I stepped into my power as a woman, and I will use my experience to help other women, hopefully protecting them from being hurt the way I was.

The other sad part is Kasey was not the only woman he was talking to. I saw a picture of Kasey's children and realized those kids were not the pictures of the kids he had shown me days prior. He had been talking to another woman with a sweet, little boy with blond hair and blue eyes. I looked at this child, thinking how cute he was because it was a "friend's" child. However, looking back now, I feel sorry for that woman and her child. They were looking for a wonderful man to have in their lives, and they found a nightmare instead. Anyone who uses women is disgusting but even more than that, a man who exploits women and their children for gain is one of the most horrendous things a human being can ever do. Adults are one thing, but the children should have never been involved. Only monsters go after children.

Monsters don't live in our closets or under our beds but in them. It's time we stand together and take the monsters down.

14

BREADCRUMBS

We cannot control who comes into our lives so much as we cannot control where the wind blows or if the ocean currents shift so much, it knocked me on my butt. Ahh, sitting on the shore right now would be amazing, but I'm sitting in my bed instead. I did, however, get knocked on my butt once when I was visiting my friend, and we decided to go to the beach.

I was getting pretty good at doing yoga, and I stood like a tree while on the beach. I was hollering for my friend to turn around, but she didn't hear me. Just then a wave crashed into me and knocked me off balance. When the wave did this, I fell into a hole in the ocean floor. My back popped out of place, and I was drowning until she helped pull me out of the water. I was only on the shoreline, but the waves were powerful. They were hitting me in the face, causing me to choke. Every time the current pulled away, I fought to get air; then when they came back in, I braced myself for the assault. I kept calling for my friend until she heard me. When she finally realized what was happening, she ran over to help me and said, *"Kell, are you okay?"* I said *"No,"* and she hoisted me out of the water like a superhero would do. Then she ran to get help from a lifeguard. He carried me from the beach all the way up to the car. I couldn't walk, and my breathing hurt from my back being out.

This is what my relationship with JJ was like. At first, it was good. Sitting on the beach with him was peaceful, and I enjoyed looking at him walking around in his trunks. I mean the guy had a really cute butt. I didn't mind whether he was 280 pounds or 160 pounds. I was there for him. I loved him unlike anyone else I'd ever been with before. He was my husband for better or for worse. However, I'm going to be honest; I just wish he would have kept his you know what in his pants and didn't cheat on me with women who were willing to bed down with my husband because they were desperate or vice versa. This is like the waves trying to drown me. It was like the abuse he constantly exposed me to. I needed someone to pull me out of the abuse just like my friend pulled me out of the ocean. I needed someone to be the steady foundation when I started to find my footing.

Abusive cycles

The stages of love bombing are as follows:

Stage one: Love Bomb

Stage two: Devaluing

Stage three: Discarding

Stage four: Hoover

At first, JJ showered me with love, this is called love bombing. He put me on a pedestal, pretending I was the most cherished woman he had ever met. The only one who had ever given him a chance to be his true self. One time we were talking, and he told me he married his first ex-wife, Karen, because he loved his oldest daughter, which he had adopted. He said he loved Mara more than Karen, he loved when she called him *"Dada"* when she was a toddler. He mentioned he never wanted to lose her, so he married her mother. That's when he told me I was the only woman he'd ever loved or trusted. I was the only one he could be himself around.

Of course, I took his touching words to heart. I was happy to be that person for him, happy to be the person he wanted to be himself around. I was glad he could open up and talk to me. I knew he loved Mara; the writing was all over his face. There was just something about her that lit up his world, but the lights faded; that's when I realized everything he was telling me was a big, fat lie. He didn't trust any woman. He was only interested in using the women in his life. JJ used us, and then he punished us for what someone else had done to him in the past. It's evident when I reflect on everything I've experienced with him. I don't believe anyone is safe around him, especially if he doesn't get his way.

It's unfortunate, but he had Mara there to control Karen while she was little. And if we are being honest, Karen used Mara to control JJ. It's a pretty low parenting approach if you ask me, as Mara got stuck in the middle. Then there is me who JJ "trusted." He knew I was getting closer with Mara, so he knew he had to keep me around. He was a Disneyland dad to the kids so they would like to come over to the house. He even did this with me in the love-bombing stage. I picked up on a few things but quickly brushed it aside when I gave him the "benefit of the doubt." I wish I was never taught to give the "benefit of the doubt." If I wouldn't have learned this as I grew up, I would have never been with JJ. I learned my feelings and emotions don't matter if I'm going to hold someone else accountable. Doing this caused me to excuse his less-than-stellar behavior in life and put myself last.

Then came the second part of JJ's abuse cycle: he devalued me. As you can see at the end of the love-bombing stage, JJ had already started conditioning me for devaluation. The things he would do to me deeply hurt me. This was my husband who promised to love and cherish me until death do we part, but he was trying to put me to death. I would greet him at the door when he came home, and he would meet me with a flat response. He would say *"hi"* and walk right by me. I stood there trying to greet him and give him a warm welcome into our home, but he couldn't get away from me fast enough. This was followed by hours of silence while he conversed with his affair partner over Instagram. He would laugh and giggle as he messaged with her and other women, but when I asked what he was laughing at, he would show me a meme.

JJ wouldn't talk to me because I wouldn't give in to all his wants. I wouldn't do it because I no longer had the money or patience to finance his immaturity. His need to feel powerful was suffocating me. I mean this is a man who skipped his daughter's graduation to show me a camper, then he tried to bully me into signing finance papers so the finance manager at the dealership could run my numbers. I couldn't believe this is where we were sitting. I wanted to sit in the Jeep and listen from the parking lot but he wasn't interested since he wasn't given a ticket to get into the graduation.

I thank God for testing me to cut JJ off in the finance area. I physically felt as though I had a devil and angel sitting on my shoulders. One was the devil encouraging me to sign the papers just so JJ would shut up about the Teardrop Camper he had picked out, and the other was an angel from God, telling me to stand my ground. I had simply asked what a "rough payment" would look like to purchase this camper. The next thing I know, JJ was pressuring me to sign papers for my numbers to be run so the finance manager could give me an "estimate." I was perturbed. I stood my ground and said he didn't need my numbers to give me a rough estimate. The finance manager could tell this was going south really quickly so he stepped out of the office so we could talk.

At this point, JJ tried to wear me down to which I didn't budge. I was merely trying to show interest in what he was interested in. However, I had zero interest in purchasing some dumb camper I was never going to use. I'm not into camping, and if I were to go camping, I would much rather take a tent. There's just something about sleeping under the stars in a tent versus a camper so I made it clear I was on a cash-only plan, no matter the picturesque road trips and vacations he had visually painted for me. He was no Picasso, and I wasn't buying what he was selling. I told him I was never financing anything for him again after I got his Jeep for him, and that's what I meant. He always needed me to finance his stupidity, and I was done being his hostage.

After this experience, I'm guessing you might be guessing what happened next. If you guessed he discarded me for a while, you'd be right. He didn't speak to me for at least a week after I didn't buy his dumb affair camper. I call it this because when I spoke to his affair partner, Kasey, she made it clear she didn't want to be the other woman.

We had a pleasant conversation, and she also informed me that he had told her his elaborate plan of how he was going back home to buy this camper, and he would bring it the next time he came to Wisconsin to visit. Well, when he showed back and didn't have it, this threw up some red flags for her. She mentioned it was at this point, she started questioning the stories he had been telling her. She said his stories were not matching up, so she did a background check with her friend, and this is when she found me. I had actually just made my Facebook profile public, so this is how we started communicating. The sad thing is she wasn't the only woman contacting me because she was trying to figure out JJ's lies. I was proud of myself for sticking to my gut instincts and not giving in to him.

Lastly, JJ discarded me when Kasey and I confronted him. Cowards like JJ don't like being held accountable, no matter how awful he was to us ... to me. He made up excuses to people like I *"treated him like a roommate,"* but he wouldn't talk to me or work with me. He went to bed by 7:30 so he could get up early to go to the gym and post pictures from the gym. He also said *"I wanted a big house,"* but he was the one who kept sending me pictures and pressuring me to buy a bigger house than his ex-wife Karen because he couldn't stand that she had a bigger house than us. I didn't care about the size of the house.

He also said he cheated on me because he was *"done."* I think this was my favorite excuse he had. He was "depressed," so he cheated on me. This excuse is so lame, it's laughable. Depression isn't something I laugh at because I've dealt with it myself, but he used this to deflect and tried to make it depression's fault he cheated. From my experience, a truly depressed person doesn't go and cheat; a loser does. Someone who is bored because they don't want to step up to be the husband they promised to be does this because it's much easier to live life in a fantasy world in Wisconsin than fix your actual problems in Indiana. It's easier to run away with your tail between your legs than man up to fix your issues and make a difference in your wife's life.

This is how the abuse cycle went for years and went on while I fought for JJ. I would have walked through fire to save his life, but in the end, I chose to see what he was showing me. I chose to listen to Kasey when she said, *"I saw his Instagram account filled with messages from other women."* The flattery, the trips, the dates, and all the things I had begged for, he just gave to other women. He never appreciated me as his wife. I did everything I could have to make his life better until the day I gave him back to God and chose myself. I told God I couldn't do it anymore, and I gave JJ back to him. I didn't want him anymore. I didn't want to lose my marriage, but I also didn't want to completely lose myself from loving someone who never cared about me in the first place.

The breadcrumbs stopped coming. The small piece of candy for Valentine's Day, a meme for my birthday, and an anniversary card with JJ's signature scribbled on it. I no longer had to nag him to tell me Happy Mother's Day for four days straight or make our anniversary something special. You know, on our eleventh anniversary, he went on another affair weekend with another woman in Kentucky. He told me he was volunteering with a veteran's group to help a man who was suicidal. He said he was helping the wife and the vet's friends check him into the VA for help. He turned his phone off and said he would be out of his service area, but I knew what that meant. It meant he didn't want to be bothered. Knowing him from what Kasey had said, he was getting trashed on Jameson Irish Whiskey and having himself a good, old time. I mean, I don't blame him for getting drunk, cheating on a wife like me. Your mental state has to be pretty shaky to do someone like me wrong because no one else would put up with or love you like I did.

Oh, and if you're dating JJ now, and he leaves really early in the morning to go hiking with the dogs to leave you home for "alone time," beware because he's probably meeting another woman. He did this to me almost every Saturday after I suggested we should go hiking on the weekends. He doesn't have his own ideas, but he will be sure to steal yours and act like they were his. Be careful because he likes to copy people's personalities because he doesn't have one of his own. He's scared of himself, so he creates someone new depending on the audience he has. It's not about you; it's about who he is too afraid to be, and putting on a facade is the only way he knows to get validation from those around him, especially in public.

15

NEW EYES, OLD VIEWS

Have you ever gone back to visit your favorite place after a long absence? Do you notice how the wind feels, the air smells, the crash of the ocean, how the sand feels as you squish it between your toes, but something feels off? It feels like you have to slide backward a bit before you move forward. You have to grieve what was before you can move forward. I can understand these feelings. The person I traveled with to my favorite place last time was no longer to be found. It feels as though this person has passed away, or they are simply gone from your life. In my case, he was a big, fat fake mirroring my personality until he could no longer keep up with my personal growth. For whatever reason, he is no more. It's good to soak in the moment. This is your moment to appreciate the time you had together, and it's also a time to acknowledge the grief that comes with moving on, even if we would rather have time stand still.

On my recent trip to Myrtle Beach, South Carolina, I found myself in this position. I spent a great deal of time soaking in the moments. I absorbed all the emotions from the past and celebrated all the new memories too. Every single moment seemed like there was a lesson for me to learn. Overwhelmingly, it was made clear to me that in those places where old memories were made, I needed to acknowledge them and feel the loss. More importantly, it was okay for me to press forward, making new memories. It felt okay for me to experience Myrtle Beach the way I needed to. I loved this new perspective. We were not meant to live in the past because that is no longer our future.

Myrtle Beach is my happy place! If you were to find me in the summer on any day I'm not working at summer camp, you could find me there. There's something about sitting on the shore, listening to the waves crash and go back out, that soothes my soul. Everything in my life could be crumbling before me but when I step onto the beach, it's like I'm walking into an alternate universe. It's my safe place where no matter what has gone wrong that day, it ceases to bother me anymore.

The beach is my little piece of heaven on earth. I had two choices when moving on from my marriage. I could allow my past to dictate how I see these present moments in my life, or I could take each moment as they come, enjoying the gift I've been given. I held the power in my hand just as you do. I know it's not easy processing and moving on, but the question is will you allow the past to put you in a cage where you are stuck forever, ceasing to move forward? Or will you learn to appreciate your new life and seize every moment there is to have?

I'm going to choose the latter. It's weird going to old places with old friends and knowing someone else once graced us with his presence there, but now that person could care less about us because we no longer offer something he can use us for. The most powerful thing about leaving someone behind is realizing the only position they held was holding you back. I took a vacation by myself to a friend's house, and I didn't allow my past to trap me. I decided to take my life back, knowing this was the second chance I needed at life. I get to live my life the way I want and take the vacations I've always dreamed of.

It's true, I set a goal to take a vacation every quarter part of the year. I achieved that goal in February 2023. It felt amazing to design a life I wanted, and I get to see the world on my terms. This big, beautiful ball called the world was created for me to explore, and I'm just getting started.

Your life can be whatever you make it so get out there and live the life you want.

16

PRAYER

I spent many nights sobbing on my couch, staring at the crucifix above my poorly painted front door. It's kinda funny if you think about it: after JJ's father died, he decided it would be a good idea to paint everyone's name on the door. We even had all the kids' friends sign it when they came over. We said everyone who came into our home was family. I guess you could say this is one of the things I loved about JJ. He would do these off-the-wall ridiculous things that no other wife would have let fly, but then there was me. I was doing my best to honor the person he was and the warmer environment we were trying to create for our family.

Honestly, this is why I fell in love with JJ. He had this charisma about him no one I had ever met had. He seemed extremely caring about his family and taking care of everyone around him. He seemed like the type of father to his kids I had always imagined raising a family with. The way he looked at his kids was the way I had imagined my husband would be smiling at the kids we would one day have together.

But as life would have it, dreams fade. Life is not a fairy tale, or the feelings you feel for someone are not always real. Don't get me wrong; JJ and I had good times, but they were never real. They were real from my side, but each of those moments, from his side, were manipulated to keep me in chaos. He was always trying to coerce me into something so he could be happy without taking into account how I felt. He won't ever be happy because he has a giant hole in his heart that is unfillable. The chaos created was to keep me in a tailspin so I never knew which way was up. This is what cognitive dissonance does to someone, keeping them so confused they don't know which way is up.

This brings me to JJ's promises. He promised he was open to having kids with me. He was diagnosed with cancer when we had only been dating for eight and a half months. He knew how much I wanted children, and he promised me no matter what, we would have "our day" to have our own children after we dropped his girls off at their grandparents' house. His visitation weekend was finished and it was time for them to return to their biological mother. I was looking out the window, watching the world pass by, as I had tears streaming down my face. Everything in my body hated leaving them behind. I couldn't stand letting life go on without them. It was early in our relationship, and the love I felt for those girls was nothing I'd felt before. Only seeing them every other weekend was a cross I never wanted to have to carry. It was mine, and I did.

There's still time. As I write this down, I'm watching the movie titled *I Can Only Imagine*. I watched this movie with JJ and remember every moment of watching this with him. I remember the tears, the laughter, and the testimony at the end. It was a movie I know brought healing not only to myself but to him, too. Mostly, I know as I'm writing this, he can still be the dad God chose him to be. I choose to believe the kids I wanted were born in Heaven because I loved them so incredibly much. I know, most people in my position wouldn't care about the person who hurt them most in this world, but I still believe in him as I type these words. I know I should give up on him, but I still have hope he can improve for the better.

The room I prayed most in my house, besides my front room, was my kitchen. I prayed for that man more than anyone I ever have in my life. I didn't even pray for myself the way I prayed for JJ. They say people cross our path for a reason, and I've asked God why, A LOT. I mean I have gone back and forth with God so many times about why JJ crossed paths with me, and I didn't understand. I didn't understand why I had to be obliterated the way I was. I not only had the trauma of being married to an abusive husband, but I was a stepmother who was subjected to abuse by his ex-wife. She wanted to control my life as well, and I refused to give into her childish antics. She's an adult bully, and I tolerated her nonsense for a period of time. I did this to protect my kids and "keep the peace." To be completely transparent, "keeping the peace" is BS. It's something dysfunctional families teach so they don't have to respect your boundaries. I put myself last in every aspect of the word, but that time has passed. I will no longer put myself last or walk on "eggshells."

I will no longer put myself last because I never felt like anyone saw me. I was the invisible woman and felt like I had to be perfect all the time. Let's be real, perfectionism is boring. No one likes a person who is perfect and has it all together. I sure didn't. But nevertheless, our paths crossed for a reason. To be completely honest, I never wanted to date a man who was divorced, let alone had children. He was the package deal in every aspect of the word.

When I chose him, I disrespected my boundaries. I stepped over boundaries that were not there because I didn't know how to keep them in place. I didn't know how to choose me first because I was always chasing people and things that wouldn't chase me back. I don't do this anymore.

I finally figured out why JJ and his "Jerry Springer" family were placed in my life. It was so I could heal the inner child wounds I had. I wasn't aware I had these wounds, but I did. I had a lot of them, and JJ plus the crazy situation he created in his life eventually exposed everything that was broken in mine.

I put JJ and our family first so many times, I became invisible. I was the one who needed healing just like he did. I just didn't use my pain to harm him or our family the way he hurt me or the way his extended family hurt me.

I chose to forgive him, and them, and trust God through every prayer I said. It's out of my hands and carefully placed in God's hands. He knows what to do.

I'm so thankful God showed me who they are so I could heal the wounds deep within my soul. I only hope they can learn how to heal, too, so they can have a better life now and for the generations to come.

17

TRAPPED

And Yahweh said, "I have indeed seen the oppression of My people who are in Mitsrayim, and have heard their cry because of their slavedrivers, for I know their sorrows. "And I have come down to deliver them from the hand of the Mitsrites, and to bring them up from that land to a good and spacious land, to a land flowing with milk and honey, to the place of the Canaanites and the Hittites and the Amorites and the Perizzites and the Hiwwites and the Yebusites. (Exodus 3:7-8, The Catholic Study Bible. Third edition).

I can imagine at some point in your life you may have asked God a variety of questions. Here are some of mine, and maybe you've asked Him something similar:

Why did my path cross with his?

What was the meaning of the damage he caused?

Why did he abuse me?

Why can't he love himself?

Why does he hate me so much?

What happened to him to make him so cruel?

Why is he so empty inside?

Why did he lie to me about having children?

Why did he want me to be the stepmother to his children if he was going to hurt me?

Why was I chosen for this pain?

Why was I trusted with this pain?

I filled countless pages with these types of questions. It's like I wanted God to hop on His spiritual phone and call me. Heaven isn't very far away. There are days I just wanted to die and go be with Him but on this day, I wanted direct answers, immediately. I needed God to answer me. What I didn't realize until now is He needed me to heal before He could answer me.

He needed me to grow through the process. He needed me to learn to trust Him before I could be trusted with the answers. He needed a disciple who would use the answers for good, someone with a heart after Jesus. He needed someone who begged to learn how to love like Jesus before she could handle the caliber of these answers. God needed a warrior who would charge through a fiery meadow, wielding a sword covered in holy armor and shouting the truth no matter how frightening the journey.

Prayers answered

As I grew, God began to answer my prayers or so I thought. At the time, I had been inviting JJ to go to church with me for seven years. I prayed he would grow to love God the same way I had started to. I hoped he would grow in faith and pray with me. He eventually converted to Catholicism, but he didn't actually do it for the right reasons. Earlier, I had considered divorcing him because of his drinking. The next thing I knew he enrolled in Rite of Christian Initiation for Adults. This is a class non-Catholics can take to convert to Catholicism. I attended most of these classes with him because I wanted to grow with him. It was a good refresher for me, but he should have paid closer attention.

He appeared serious about turning his life around and growing with me in our marriage, reading scripture with our family and attended Mass with me weekly. I felt like one of my biggest prayers had been answered. I had a Catholic husband, and we could grow in our journey together. I felt like this is what God wanted for me, and He had his hand in it. However, I soon realized JJ did this to keep me from leaving him and from filing for divorce because I thought he was turning his life around, but this was short-lived.

He should have paid closer attention because the things he was doing to me, God hates. God hates when you abuse people and commit adultery. You're not supposed to covet what someone else has and by becoming Catholic, JJ condemned himself. I'm stating this fact to show you how desperate he was to keep me trapped. I was his "toy," and he wanted to keep me because he earned me fair and square, but he was so desperate to keep me in this mess he put himself in a worse position.

Rescue

I know I'm not the one who was put here to rescue JJ; that is God's job, but I'm concerned for his soul. I'm concerned about where he will end up. By trapping me in a situation that I've broken free from, he is still trapped. I actually think he's worse off. His plan was to keep me as his main source of egocentric supply while he had fantasy affairs staying in a camper in Wisconsin on the weekends, but once exposed his sins came to light.

I say this because I don't understand why he went to the lengths to keep me in his life when he really only wanted to use me. Why not get a divorce and not put yourself into a situation where you're going to be condemned?

I'm guessing I'm not the only one that has asked these questions, but to see the extreme lengths someone will take so they can maintain control over someone else is insane. Trying to control what someone does is insanity and to live within these empty shells.

I can't say I'm surprised though. I went into this relationship as a soft-hearted young woman who wanted to be loved. A woman who decided to love a man and his four children. One of which he hid from the world because of the reality of this child, where some of his deepest fears would be exposed. This relationship not only helped me grow and learn as the years advanced, but I developed knowledge in the area of narcissism I knew I never wanted to know. You could even say I have a "PhD" in narcissism. Narcissism is sickening, and I hope you never have to experience it.

Mindset

In the time I spent alone, trying to understand why I was treated this way, I learned more about who JJ was. He constantly complained that his friends don't check in on him, or his exes just think he's a walking bank account that's supposed to barf out money whenever they demand it. He even got mad after people did not wish him "Happy Birthday" on social media when he removed his information from his account. He wanted everyone to remember his birthday without a reminder; this was coming from an adult, not a child. Talk about manipulation and an ego trip. This was manipulation at its finest, yet when I would do something special for his birthday and I kept it between us, he would get mad. He wanted all the attention and wouldn't recognize anything I did because he didn't receive public acknowledgment. JJ even removed his profile for a while to see if anyone would notice. Oh my goodness! What a baby.

This is the stuff I dealt with. I tried harder to make him happy, and every time I tried harder, he gave less effort. I got memes for my birthday. MEMEs ... the grown-up who was complaining about not getting any attention for his birthday sent me a meme. He couldn't be bothered to get me flowers or a card or, dare I say, give me a birthday present to show any "love" or appreciation he had for me.. JJ, you reap what you sow. And you, sir, have sowed seeds of death over your life. No one wants to celebrate you if you refuse to celebrate others.

During this time, I started attending conferences that would challenge me to become the best person I could be. I learned about makeup, copyright, business, etc. I learned about how I needed my life to change and how I feel safe. I was actually happy to be the most uneducated person in the room. This made me happy because I could learn from those I just met.

Good husbands and wives want their spouses to be happy. They want them to enjoy life and be content with where they are and, dare I say, they are even more happy when one or both are trying to improve life for the better for their family. I was the wife who would encourage my husband but OH LORD ... how dare I go and grow. How dare I start investing in my own life when my confidence starts showing up.

At this point in my life, JJ, started making comments about how he "hated" this coach or that coach who was helping me improve my life. I would always end up apologizing because this is what he wanted. What I came to realize was that JJ didn't hate my coaches, but he hated what they were teaching me. He hated that I was wearing makeup because he would get mad when I walked by someone, and they were paying more attention to me than him. He also didn't like that my confidence was getting stronger, and I no longer begged for his validation. I didn't want his validation. I no longer thought he was the most special person in my life because I was growing.

When I first met JJ, I thought he was this wonderful guy and how lucky I was to be his wife. I did my best to honor him as a man. The way I looked at him I had never looked at any other person before. What I came to realize though was the more I invested in myself, the more I realized he was giving me the short end of the stick. He didn't treat me like a wife. The man I was so thankful to have as mine had nothing to offer me, and I learned I was the man and woman in the home. I was the husband and the wife and as much as I loved JJ, it was time for me to start opening my eyes to the man I was really with. I can't say he's a man at all. A real man wouldn't treat me like garbage or abuse me. He would take care of me, which JJ never did. This is why he hated my coaches because they exposed everything he worked so hard to hide from me.

When you take care of your mindset and invest in yourself, it's hard for people to take you for granted. You are the one who holds the key for people to access you.

18

LOSS

Loss seems tragic.

Loss seems permanent.

Sometimes loss even parades itself around as a punishment.

Loss seems to define every aspect of our lives when we're in the thick of it.

Loss is a loss.

It is more of an experience and not a definition.

I'm going to take a wild guess here that you may or may not agree with me. You may be in a situation that seems unbearable. It appears as though it is sucking the very energy from your being. You are begging God for an extended vacation, hoping something or someone comes to rescue you from this test, but nothing or no one does.

You are sitting in your bed, covered up with your favorite cozy blanket and sipping your peppermint mocha coffee as you peer out the window. This is while tears stream down your face as you wonder where your life went wrong.

You might be revisiting a situation for the millionth time, trying to make sense of it all and realizing you are never going to have all the answers. Reality hits you, and you finally realize you won't have all the pieces to know. Moving forward from that loss is tough, but staying planted in a place of uncertainty is a recipe for death.

If you're like me, then you want a sure thing. You want reassurance and know you are doing a job well done. Unfortunately, life doesn't come with a guarantee. Do know this: when you share your feelings with someone, and it appears you are losing them because of what you said, it is actually the opposite. Your life is being aligned by them losing you. It's not a loss; it's a gain. Their loss is literally your gain.

Now you might be wondering "How is this a gain?" There are several ways we could look at this. I've talked about JJ so let us use him for an example. I knew JJ for far too long, a painfully long time. I'd like to barf just thinking about it. When GOD kicked him out of my life, it was painful. I went days without sleeping because of the trauma he had inflicted on me. However, what I did not realize was when I was with him, God wouldn't bless me. He held His blessing back from me.

I know this might sound a little silly. I always thought I was a good person and God would answer my prayers, but not when I wasn't aligned with His plan. JJ was not aligned with His plan while with me.

I was out in the world living Kelly's plan. My plan sucked, but I thought I had to solve every little problem, so I extended myself so far out there was literally no room for God. Gasp! I'm embarrassed to admit it, but God was trying to help me in 2011 with a $200 gift card from the grocery store. I prayed so hard I'd win the card. The day came, and I received the call, which was a bad one. JJ and I were driving the girls back to their mother's house. I was upset because I loved having them around, and I just wanted them to be with me that day. I didn't want to share them with anyone. I had also been receiving an insane amount of calls because someone used my information to get ahead in life, and my phone rang twenty-four hours a day nonstop. I was grouchy, upset, and peeved ... that's when the phone call came in from the local newspaper that was giving away the $200.

First, I couldn't figure out how to answer the phone because it was ringing through my car speakers. Side note: I don't know who invented this on the car, but I dislike you very strongly because this tech-challenged person could never figure out how to work it correctly. Plus, I wasn't driving so I couldn't see all the buttons to make a selection. By the time I figured out how to answer the phone, I was so flustered, I said hello, and the lady gave this long speech about where she was calling from (another spam call), and I then hung up the phone because I was annoyed.

This is what happens when you let life get to you. You become insanely unhappy, and no one wants to be around you. The second JJ hung up the "spam" call, I remembered the contest I entered.

That loss was a little painful and tragic. At the time I had no money, and my credit card was maxed out. I needed that money, but I got a lesson instead. I feel the person who got the call after me was meant for them. They needed it more than me. I had it in my head that I didn't need God's help at all, and I could do it on my own. I wanted to do everything on my own, and you see how that worked out.

This is why God was not blessing me. This is why my plan was not working. This is why my entire life that year and the next ten absolutely sucked. I wasn't supposed to be with JJ, and I missed all the signs to avoid him. JJ was blocking my blessings, and I wasn't going to get anything extra until his scrubby, freeloading arse got out of my life, once and for all. Once he left, I had unexpected checks come in the mail. I also got a job with the freedom I had been dreaming about, and the debt I had when I was with him, I paid almost all of that off too.

So, you see, losing my marriage was a big loss. It felt like my life was crumbling underneath me, but the blessing that came with that loss was way better. God and I have a much better relationship. Actually, I do my best to keep God in the driver's seat at all times because He is more prepared than I'll ever be.

I know He wants to be in my life, and He doesn't mind controlling my car. Plus, He has to be the safest driver around.

Why hasn't God moved yet?

Have you had a loss so big you question God about it? No really, I mean you question Him with all the anger, fury, and might you have welled up in your body. This anger feels like if it doesn't spill out of you, then you might as well be at death's door.

I'm not proud to say it, but I was irate with God after my marriage came crashing down. I blamed Him for everything. He would remind me to "stay in my lane," but that advice wasn't for me. I would scream at Him, yell profanities, and when my dogs were gone, just me in the house, I would break stuff. It didn't solve anything, but after I found the white towel JJ stole from the gym soaked in his semen, after having sex with yet another affair partner, I deserved to let my anger out.

I even wanted to call his first ex-wife and let her break stuff too upon learning the news, but I didn't. She had better things to do than sit in misery with me; besides, she already dealt with this clown before. This was my circus, and I didn't want it.

In time, I was thankful for this loss because it turned into a blessing.

REDEMPTION

19

WHO WAS I?

I've asked myself, many times, how did I end up in this relationship that turned into a marriage? I know I'm a good person with a big heart, and I put my best forward for those I love and even strangers. I'm willing to go out of my way and give someone the shirt off my back or give them money so they can get something to eat.

It's true; I opened my home many times to my kids' friends that have needed a place to stay, but there was something missing inside of me. I kept trying to fulfill myself by helping others.

This is how I ended up living a real-life horror story.

The Old Me

The old me was a sweet girl. She played with her best friend down the street, and he always had my back. I sort of lived in a bubble where most people had my back. My best friend's parents protected me and took me to soccer practice. They also invited me over for dinner and let me stay for hours on end. I didn't know the difference between good and bad in the community because, in my world, everything was good. My neighbors looked out for me.

It's true. I stopped and talked to most people when I was out and about riding my bike or taking a walk. My sister and I even disappeared into someone's house for a while because we wanted to babysit their triplets and two-year-old. My mom was irate! She grounded us because we did that, and the next time we went into the house, we told her where we were going. This was before cell phones and lazy parenting. My mom knew how to sniff us out so we might as well make sure she knew where we were going. She was not cute when she was mad. Haha!

So, in my mind, I may have had a bad day, but God gave me this gift to see the world with a silver lining. I learned to trust people until they couldn't be trusted, but I didn't know to make them earn my trust first. This would have been a much better way to live my life. Unknowingly, I trusted people who were not trustworthy.

Why?

This is why I landed in the marriage that I did. I didn't know how to properly feel people out. I didn't know what a "red" flag was and didn't know how to look within myself to know my own value or worth. I was taught to look to society and others to validate me, but I was taught the wrong way. I've learned this as I healed and have let grace grow within me.

When I attended school, I was taught to be friends with everyone and not stick up for myself. I wasn't allowed to have my own voice, which was especially confusing because I had a learning disability. The other kids would tease me but when I did stick up for myself, I got scolded by my teacher. She made me think I was wrong for having a boundary and made me apologize to the kids who were bullying me. Real nice, right? Not a great teacher. They got to bully me with zero consequences.

Then when I got into high school, my principal accused me of making fun of someone, and even though she had the wrong person, she still made me apologize for something I didn't do. I wasn't sorry. She ripped me a new one but never took responsibility for correcting the wrong person. The principal assumed she did the right thing and never found the actual girl who was responsible for the bullying. This colored my world, as I decided I had to be my own safe place at school.

From this moment on, I began to shut myself off from the world, as I knew I had to protect myself. The boys I dated in high school also were not the best. They were individuals with low self-esteem who took their anger and insecurities out on me.

One time, I was wearing a Halloween costume to high school, and the top broke. My cleavage was exposed a bit because I was dressed as a Greek goddess; it only showed as much as a bikini swimsuit would. My boyfriend at the time became irate because his classmates were commenting on my breasts. I felt ashamed of myself, but I never should have been. He was the one being callous toward my situation. He was mean about the incident, and it hurt me deeply. This is how my series of misguided relationships started. I'm not happy I had to learn this way about relationships and self-worth, but I eventually learned what was and what was not a healthy relationship.

"Red" Flags and signs of an unhealthy relationship

Here are some examples that you may benefit from knowing:

- Silent treatment
- Psychological abuse
- Emotional abuse
- Missed events because you didn't comply with their demands or bullying
- Nights without a real hug or kiss (just him/her placing their body on you while you hug them)
- Lies
- Confusion (Cognitive Dissonance)
- Financial abuse
- Being used for "babysitting"
- Love-bombing

- Projection (Blamed for things your abuser is actually doing)
- Deflection
- Alcohol abuse
- Being cheated on daily (Physically, emotionally, or this can be by messaging the opposite sex without your knowledge)
- Refusal to let you see or use their phone
- They are on their phone consistently.
- Domestic violence
- Gaslighting
- Triangulation
- Belittlement
- Sexual abuse
- You are silenced when you attempt to speak.
- They become angry or aggressive when you express yourself or while holding them accountable.
- Gut instincts—how your body responds to a situation
- Listen to how someone talks about themselves—JJ said, "I'm an ahole but..." I defended him. Don't defend them. Listen carefully. The more you observe, the more you learn.
- They throw a fit when you spend money on yourself.
- They become upset or angry when you make your own plans/live your own life—JJ yelled at me for spending time with my mom for my birthday.
- You deny your own feelings to "keep the peace."
- You are told to "keep the peace."
- You pay all the bills.
- You are financing all the cars.
- There is an imbalance of power.
- They're attempting to control you.
- Fast moving relationship- They may say they're so in love with you and have "never felt this way about anyone."
- They are unavailable when "on a trip with the guys/girls."

Signs of a Healthy Relationship

- You feel safe
- They keep you safe.
- You can trust them.
- You can communicate with them.
- They make eye contact
- They respect your boundaries.
- They are willing to call/text you as much as you call/text them.
- You are able to be yourself.
- They accept you for who you are.
- You are able to openly share your thoughts and ideas
- You share financial responsibilities or responsibilities in general.
- They are honest
- They value you
- They celebrate you on your birthday, anniversary, or holidays
- They show affection to you.

Overcomer

These are the things I had to overcome to become the woman I am today. I had to look evil in the eye and decide I was going to push forward. Every day I woke up, I decided I was going to fight for myself. I had to keep fighting for myself because if I didn't, no one else would. I learned about the red flags and everything I had been exposed to. I even worked in a school at this time, and the red flags that existed within this corporation stuck out like a sore thumb. I couldn't put up with it any longer. The things they "stood" for were not actually upheld. Leaving this corporation was hard, but it was worth it. I wanted to work somewhere that stood for something.

I took the knowledge about all the cruel, psychological mind games I had experienced and used those to catapult me forward. I learned what they were so I would no longer be a victim, as I wanted to help those like myself. There may have been others around me who were abused like I was, but no one was talking about it. I didn't want to sweep the abuse under the rug but wanted to expose the shit out of it so no one ever had to experience what I did.

So here I am, writing this book so everyone can live a better life. I'm not backing down from the truth, even though I've been threatened by the ex-family I stayed in contact with while writing it. My ex-family said if I didn't comply with their demands, I could no longer be a part of their lives. They wanted me to keep the "family secrets" I'm no longer willing to keep. I find this amusing because I removed myself from their lives before these threats were made. I can't help that they're so insecure and controlling, they resulted in threatening me. It's sad but you might experience the same thing when you speak out. Don't give up; the truth will set you free. Literally.

20

INTO THE SHADOWS

I lie down in peace altogether, and sleep; For You alone, O Yaweh,
make me dwell in safety.
(Psalm 4:8, The Catholic Study Bible. Third Edition).

Have you ever been to a baseball game where there's that serene silence just after the ball leaves the pitcher's hand, and it catapults through the air? The ball is delivered with a swiftness to the batter's box as everyone watches to see what will happen next. Will the batter crush the ball with power and knock it out of the park or will he be a hair too slow?

This is what my everyday life was like. Imagine living every day as if you were waiting for the moment for the ball to be pitched and the assault to be launched. There was no bat or ball but instead a barrage of emotional and psychological warfare thrown at you. You must navigate each assault in order to survive, or you duck and cover. That was my life. Day in and day out, I held my breath to see if it was going to be an easy pitch kind of day or would it be a split-finger fastball kind. I never knew what was coming, and there wasn't really any way to prepare for what would be happening.

I had to come up with a plan. I was literally driving myself insane because I couldn't get him to stop the reckless behavior I was witnessing. When JJ was asleep in the house, I would go through his vehicles. He had a variety through the years when we were married, as he liked having a "new toy" every couple of years. He wanted to have the best or the best of what I could afford because we ran my credit score for whatever reason I was presented with. You can fill in the blanks. If you know his ex, well, then you can take a guess at what he said.

This meant I had to find hiding spots within these vehicles for shiny vessels that contained liquids that didn't belong in the vehicle. I hope you're picking up what I'm putting down here. This would be the part of the book where my English teacher would tell me to read between the lines.

Once I was done looking through his vehicles, then I would dump the contents out and throw it in the trash. I'd make sure the bottles were broken and couldn't be reused again. One morning, I wasn't so lucky, and a shiny glass vessel fell out of the back of his black, Toyota 4-Runner. I tried to catch the vessel before it hit the ground, but it was too late. Ahh, I missed the "pitch," and I sliced my thumb open. It was a clean cut but the blood was gushing out.

I know I sound like an overzealous wife at this point, and maybe I was, but I was doing what I knew to keep people safe. I prayed so much about the contents in these vessels, I was convinced God was getting tired of the same prayers day after day. Heck, I would have made a direct call and told me to get over it already, but I couldn't. I knew I had to take a stand, even though at some point, that curveball was going to come at me.

Just imagine thinking you had a nice place to stash your liquid "valuables" and when you went to retrieve them, they were gone. I'm sure he used some choice words. That might be what you'd have done, too. I don't know, I wasn't usually around or maybe it didn't matter because there was another vessel stashed somewhere else. That was until I started feverishly cleaning the house.

The house was a puzzle for hidden vessels. I actually do not enjoy puzzles, but this was one I was eager to solve. It involved the safety of others so the search continued. I searched closets, drawers, under the beds, in the access wall that was only for leaks under the tub (eyes rolling here), in the garage, in the toolboxes, above the cabinets in the laundry room, under the clothes in the laundry baskets, behind the shed in the backyard, under the wood pile, inside our furniture in the living room, and much more. Anywhere these vessels could fit, there was something shoved there. Those little airport-sized vessels were the worst. I also found a few boxes of condoms that male "visitors" had left at the house and in the vehicles. Supposedly, this was because they did not want their multiple girlfriends finding out that they had more than one woman in their life. I called bs on this but honestly there was no having a discussion with someone who was never awake when I was home, ever. I went to work, and he was asleep. I arrived home from work, and he was asleep. This continued for years.

My marriage had turned into me babysitting the very person who had promised to love, honor, and cherish me until death do we part. It was just me, by myself, day in and day out. Thankfully, this is no longer my story, and I can stand in the light, leaving the shadows behind. I'm no longer scared of the truth or anyone threatening me to keep secrets I don't want to keep.

Freedom is mine!

21

UNHINGED

On my wedding day, I was a smitten twenty-five-year-old bride. I thought it was JJ and I against the world. We were going to accomplish everything we set our minds to and nothing less. I imagined what our lives would look like together.

I dreamt up names for our future children and what it would feel like to hear the pitter patters of their little feet coming down the hallway. I couldn't wait to give my babies their morning snuggles. I couldn't wait to meet these little people I loved so much but had yet to meet. I even wondered what their little voices would sound like, what "Momma" would sound like coming from them, even though my step-kids were already calling me "Mommy." It was so cute, and I couldn't wait to add to our lives.

Life was so beautiful on May 16, 2008 when I said, "I do." He was everything I thought I wanted in this life. I thought he embodied everything I wanted in a husband. He appeared confident, fun, adventurous, organized, dedicated, empathetic, caring, and a committed family man. I wanted what I didn't have growing up, and I thought I found it in him. I was so wrong; he was none of those things. He wasn't the man I wanted to raise kids with anymore. My head understood me, but my heart didn't.

Whiskey, vodka, beer, and more

Three years down the road, our life was a disaster.

This is the hard part. I don't want to tell you any of this because I have fought for so long to keep it a secret. I kept it a secret because it was my only option. I did what I was taught to do and kept the secrets because I didn't know how JJ was going to react if I told someone. I didn't know what side of his personality would come out.

It's sad. Most of my adult life was spent in survival mode. Every day, I was living to keep him happy and keep myself safe. I did what I could to keep everyone in the house happy, except for me. For me, happiness was fleeting. I was really good at putting on a smile and looking for the good in everything, but eventually, that mentality ran out.

If I wasn't being yelled at because I didn't give him money or have my own opinions, I would be ridiculed because I wouldn't do this or that for my step-kids. I wouldn't do exactly as their moms demanded. It was easy for them to hide how they treated me when it wasn't directly in front of the kids. I didn't care what they wanted; it was my house. It was my life. I was the one who was working to pay for every-thing, and I took care of my stepchildren for most of the time they were in my house. My house, my life. I wasn't going to buckle because Karen was having a meltdown, which she often did and still does. When I stood my ground with her, she literally lost her mind. People are possessions to her and things to control. She's careless and self-involved. She doesn't care about anyone but herself and didn't even want my stepson around his sisters, also trash-talking him when he was playing football. At least I showed up for him. She just wanted to pick him apart, as picking people apart is a sport for her.

Everywhere I turned, there was a critic. The worst part was this filled me with anxiety, depression, and irritable bowel syndrome. I'm serious. I could poop on demand. Some days, I even had suicidal thoughts. I didn't think anyone would miss me if I was gone. My family by marriage has proven this to be true.

I thought I was marrying the love of my life and creating something together but instead, I prayed for God to take my life. I couldn't do it anymore.

Almost every day I came home, JJ was drunk. He would be passed out in his easy chair, drooling. I couldn't stand looking at him. I would watch him while he slept to make sure he didn't get sick, or choke, and I'd wipe the drool from his face. Sometimes I wished the cancer would have taken him so I didn't have to endure the pain I went through. He had surgery to remove all his testicular cancer cells, so he likes to tell people he beat cancer often. I heard him tell the story so many times, it was nauseating. Plus, he tells this joke about how he turns one way or another because it's a little heavier as he still has a nut on that side of his body, so lame. Listening to him made me dumber some days, and other days it made me a bit wiser because I was hip to his patterns. I even recognized when someone discovers who he really is, he leaves the group of friends he has and creates a whole new group so he can use them, and no one will be any wiser to what he's doing.

I wasn't thankful at first, but I'm thankful now that his body produces sperm like that of a toddler. These are the words JJ told me his doctor used to describe his sperm count. I'm thrilled they are weak and so unintelligent they can't find their way out of his scrotum. And if his doctor did cut his sperm duct, I'm thankful. Heck, even if JJ got a vasectomy without telling me and his nut was basically a jail for his sperm, because God knew we shouldn't have kids together, I'm still thankful. He did me a favor being self-absorbed. Only the ignorant would have wanted us to have kids together, and that's pretty much anyone who wouldn't acknowledge the torture he was inflicting upon me.

It didn't matter how much he drank or the excuses he came up with, JJ will always be a broken and lost soul until he decides to change things. He won't improve his life until he allows God to change it.

Why me?

I know, I know. There have been so many times I've asked myself why he picked me. I didn't ask myself because life is so grand. I asked myself this because he tried to destroy my life. I may have had to give everything up, but it was a lot better than being trapped in a cage with him. When I gave everything up, I regained my independence. I regained my freedom I'd been missing for so long.

The first thing I learned to understand was I wasn't picked because I was weak. I was picked because I was empathetic, caring, a strong role model, accomplished, and driven among other things. People like JJ are insecure, and they prey on people like me and possibly you. If you have unhealed childhood trauma and you are around someone like him, he will exploit the cracks you have exposed.

What are the "cracks," you ask? Allow me to educate you. The cracks you have are emotional wounds and triggers predators prey on. They appear empathetic, as though they care about your life, but what they are actually doing is listening so they can later use those childhood wounds to trap you.

My wound

How JJ exploited my wound

An emotionally unavailable father figure who I couldn't connect with on a deep level.

He pretended to care about his children, and he behaved as a caring father figure who was deeply connected to his children.

Insecurities/Worth/Value

He manipulated my wounds to make me feel like I had to compete against others and win his love.

Codependent

He allowed me to take care of all his needs, while my needs were unmet. He allowed me to validate him while he ignored me.

Unfulfilled needs in my life

He gave me the bare minimum known as "breadcrumbs." Then taught me not to depend on him in any way, shape, or form.

My ex-fiancé cheated on me and broke my trust.

He exploited my wound by saying his two exes, the mothers of his children, cheated on him too and hurt him deeply.

How healing changed me

Healing is hard; there is no easy way around it. When JJ left and walked out of the house, I was relieved. I was no longer enslaved to him, no longer walking on eggshells. On the other hand, when he left, it was the most excruciating pain I had ever experienced in my life. Since he left, my body recognized it could finally decompress. All the trauma he put me through would now have to be slowly processed. I had to work through the love-bombing, cognitive dissonance (constant confusion), and gaslighting. My brain was addicted to him because of the trauma he inflicted upon me. The only way to go from here was down.

Withdrawal

The first thing I experienced upon my separation from JJ was the loss of sleep. I had ruminating thoughts that kept going through my mind. I didn't sleep for the first seventy-two hours that he had been gone. I needed the physical touch he would give me to reinforce his validation of me. This was the way I got a contact high from him. When he went to work or on an affair weekend, I was fine because he was gone for a short time, and I knew he would come back. However, once I knew he wasn't coming back, my mind tried to take control of the situation. I tried to figure out how I could make things better.

The second thing I noticed was I had no appetite. I couldn't get myself to eat because the guilt of not being able to fix my marriage was eating away at me. I lost eleven pounds within a week, and I had to force myself to eat and my mental health plummeted. During this time, I refused to eat so much that my blood sugar would tank, and I'd start shaking. I'd have to ask someone to grab me something sugary just to make it through to the next day. When I did eat, it was usually two hot dogs and candy from the concession stand at my step-kids' high school. It wasn't the healthiest meal, but it put something in my body. I tried to eat most days, but then I wanted to vomit because my stress was so high. I didn't know what would become of my life, and everything was happening so fast.

The last thing I noticed was extreme fatigue. I did my best to function in my day-to-day life, but this was a challenge. I wanted to sleep so badly, but my mind and body wouldn't let me. I jokingly asked my sister to punch me really hard in my face so I could get some sleep. This is how desperate I was to get some rest. My mental health was deteriorating, and I was so exhausted. I needed a little break and would have done anything to get some rest.

Reality check

The next step I took was facing the reality of our relationship and marriage. I took time to actively reflect on the abuse I experienced from JJ. The truth is no one wants to think the person they were married to consciously hurt them. No one wants to think multiple family members were against them, but this was my reality. I was devastated when I realized JJ never loved me, and he tortured me for game. His twisted mind needed to "win." He needed to feel like he was on top when he was actually on the bottom, wallowing in his own self-pity and dying for someone to admire and validate him.

While he put me through this torture, he would manipulate me to believe untruths about him and myself. He exploited me for personal gain. Most days, if he wanted something from me, like a vehicle, he would shower me with love-bombing. These are the only times he took me out to dinner and paid attention to me. He manipulated the situation so I would be in a good mood so he could get what he wanted. He would pamper me and treat me as though I was the most wonderful wife in the whole world; however, after he got what he wanted, he would ignore me and take his multiple affair partners for rides in the Jeep I helped purchase. I know this because multiple family members and friends told me they saw a variety of women in our black, two-door Jeep, around the city of Indianapolis, Mooresville, and Carmel.

The reality that he never wanted to be married to me as my husband but wanted access to me for what he could get was shocking. Once I acknowledged this, I battled with denial and self-doubt. I continued to question my reality as my healing continued. In my mind, I took responsibility for everything that took place, even though it wasn't my conscious choice to hurt myself. I finally came to terms that he was the monster who hurt me. He chose to hurt and use me. He chose to marry me so he could have someone to have sex with, a maid, someone to pay his bills so he could be cared for, and have a beck-and-call babysitter when he needed it so he didn't have to take care of his children. He needed someone to adore him, and I did until I didn't.

After I confronted my denial and self-doubt, I educated myself. JJ always complained about how his first ex-wife, Karen, was a narcissist. He would talk about her behavior and the cycles of behavior she exhibited. I started researching and paying attention to what a narcissist is. His complaining led me to more healing and knowledge. The more I learned about narcissism, the more I got angry. He would become irate when Karen messed with him, yet the same things she was doing to him, he did to me. He deserved it.

Emotional rollercoaster

This brings me to the next stage. This is the stage nobody wants to talk about. We might feel wrong for feeling this way when we worked so hard to hide and fix our situation by ourselves. We learned to depend on ourselves, and only ourselves, because we learned we couldn't trust anyone else, even if they told us we could.

It's anger.

We don't always want to talk about our anger.

When it comes to emotions, it's easier to get mad first. It's easier to respond with anger and let it allow us to dictate how we respond to life. Some people get cheated on and when they are treated the way I was, they might lose themselves because the pain is excru-ciating.

They might scream, break stuff, or think when they lose someone like JJ that their life is over. I'd be lying if I didn't say I was upset or that I didn't scream. It wasn't funny at the time but when I was cleaning out the house, I broke stuff. Anything I wasn't going to keep, sell, or donate got broke. I smashed it to pieces, and it felt so good. That was a bonus to having everything else left to me in the divorce. I got to take care of it the way I saw fit.

All that broken stuff got thrown in the trash right next to my broken heart. I broke stuff that meant nothing to me, and I didn't get in trouble for doing something more intense I'd like to think we only see in movies. I'm talking about when someone gets cheated on and the other person can't handle it, and bad stuff happens, I broke stuff instead. Sometimes anger is there to protect you. Sometimes it's entrusted to you to get your attention. Anger needs you to see what is going on so you can protect yourself when nobody else has your back.

Anger gave me a new lease on life. It allowed me to come to terms with what was going on and for me to wake up. It gave me the courage to keep moving forward, even when I didn't want to.

After this, I was able to start addressing my deeper pain. I started working on my own mental health, and I found a mental health professional who could help me. I realized the depression and anxiety I lived with, day in and day out, was caused by him. The torment, word salads and cognitive dissonance kept me confused. My brain didn't know how to cope so it shut down. It did what it could to protect me. I used to be ashamed of my depression and anxiety, but I overcame it. What I used to see as a weakness is one of my greatest strengths. I overcame everything I went through because of my anxi-ety. My anxiety helped me see pieces of the puzzles I would have missed if I didn't have them. Plus, it helped me to trust my instincts again. JJ gaslit me so much that I started second-guessing myself, but I know my instincts were correct.

In the end, I took charge of my healing, and I started validating myself. The old me I knew who was afraid to lose anyone let every-thing go. She stopped holding onto everyone so tightly that never wanted to be in her life. She stopped chasing the people who never loved her. She started speaking her mind and being her true self. She became me; I am the woman I am proud of. I'm proud to be me because I'm no longer trapped by my past or the people within it. I'm proud of who I am today because I no longer allow other people in society to validate me, but I validate myself. I live for God and my own validation. Beyond that, if I receive praise, it's a bonus but my worth and value no longer weigh in on what other people say about me.

22

F-BOMB MOM

Up to this point in my life, I've tried to be a good Christian. I even met with Mara, Xavier, Piper, and Zoe before I decided to write this book. Well, Mara was supposedly too exhausted to show up to meet with me, so I bought Chic-fil-a for the four of us and we talked about my plans to write this book.

I told them I was going to be writing a book about my life and everything that happened in my marriage and anything that comes to mind. They were excited and nothing else. They said they supported me and wanted to be there for me, since I had always been there for them. Piper even said she would read my book, while the other two said they wouldn't because they don't like to read. I get it; I didn't like reading at their ages either, or until the gap to my learning disability closed, and I saw the value in reading.

I was so excited to include them in this chapter of my life. I even asked them several times, "Are you sure if I write this book and do everything I need to do with it, you are good with it? Like in a year, you are not going to be mad, and this is not going to ruin our relationship?" They swore up and down this wouldn't ruin our relationship. They were proud of me for taking these steps forward.

Fast forward, eight months later, they changed their minds. They decided not to support me and told me they wanted me to change my social media presence. They tried to paint a picture as though I didn't care about them. That I didn't give them any consideration before I took this step in my life. I did though, and you can't promise to support me and then change your mind; this isn't how promises work.

When you give someone your word, you need to stick to it, no matter how hard it is and no matter who else is in your life telling you need to convince me otherwise. Once I make a decision to complete something, I stick to it. I lived scared and in fear for too many days in my life, and I refuse to live this way any longer. I'm going to be audacious and courageous in my life. If this means I have to flip a few tables, then so be it. My Father flipped tables, and so can I.

He didn't walk on eggshells around those who tried to tell Him this is how He should be living His life. No, He knew the way He was supposed to live His life, and He stepped into His purpose, and I plan on doing the same thing. I plan on following His example, and if you don't like it, then I suppose you'll be like those running out of the temple when He told them the temple wasn't a marketplace. Jesus wasn't someone who wanted to be sold on their opinions, and I'm not someone who wants to be sold on the opinion of others, especially those who were not in my shoes, to live a certain life.

Let's be honest: I only hear from my kids when they want me to show up to an event and then not post it with parts of my life that mean the most to me, or they want me to protect those who only speak to me when they're trying to show me up or criticize me.

This isn't how I'm going to live my life.

I've done my best to be a good Christian. I've tried to do all the right things, encourage people the correct way, serve my family in a way I can be proud of, and teach my kids how to lead a good life but this, honestly, has gotten me nowhere. I don't think they've heard a word I said. My role modeling days were most likely chalked up to hot air, rolling eyes behind closed doors, and them denouncing me as any kind of parent to them. At least this is how I feel. Ya know, just out here living that Stepmomma life ... well, ex-Stepmomma life now.

I gotta add all the details so someone doesn't get their britches in a bunch.

I mean, God forbid I write about my life. How rude of me to have my own life and opinion as a stepmother. Shocker! I don't know about you, but I'm not down with society's views on stepmoms. I can love my kids and get peeved at them too, just like any other parent. If you don't like my point, go get some cheese and whine. Yes, I do mean whine. Then address your woes because this momma doesn't give a rip.

I'm serious, If I don't put all the specific details and watch my step, someone is going to call, text, comment something nasty on social media, or just continue to stalk me, even though I've blocked their profiles. They'll just continue stalking me by creating new profiles.

It's cute they want to keep in contact with me, but I'm sure there's more to life than getting their g-string in a bunch over me. It's sad but true. I found a g-string on my daughter's floor when she was thirteen years old. My dog, Zeus, chewed it up, and I rewarded him for it. Thirteen-year-olds shouldn't be wearing lingerie from Victoria Secret or spending their money in a store like this. Haha, no one listened to my parenting then, but maybe they will now. Be a better parent.

Don't let your kids spend the money wherever they want just because they can.

I've caught them in so many triangle conversations, called triangulation, it's no longer funny. It's sad to think this is what my life has come to and theirs. They've learned how to manipulate and coerce people but didn't learn it from me. I'm glad I'm not the one who created that toxic legacy.

Choose well

It's true. I did what any frustrated parent would do, and I threw in the towel. I decided if my best efforts were going to be ignored, then I was going to choose myself over everyone else. I was going to start doing for myself what I always wanted someone else to do for me.

When I show up to events, take time out of my life and show up for you but you won't show up for me and behave as though I don't exist, something has to change. I'm saying this because I might not be the only one who has extended myself so far for others, I'm depleted.

I show up for others when they won't show up for me. I'm still waiting for my kids to get back to me about the family dinner from 2021. Thank goodness I didn't hold my breath. I did enjoy spending the money I had saved for the dinner that never happened. I had a nice vacation. I did the same with their birthday money and dinners. When other people don't prioritize you, then you have to prioritize yourself.

Priorities

There comes a time in life when you have to stop waiting and make things happen. Sure, the family vacation you planned might not include all the people you wanted there, but it will include the ones who want to be there. As I sit here, I'm reflecting on the vacation I took to Disney World.

Once upon a time, my kids asked me to plan this vacation for them. They wanted me to take them on the vacation because when they went with their mom, Karen, they said she did what she wanted, and they didn't get to pick what they would like to do because she was paying for it.

The thing is I did plan the trip for them, but relationships changed, and none of them went with me. I still took the trip and invited my sister and nephew to go. It was a lot less expensive on my part, and I got to have the vacation I dreamed of.

I enjoyed spending my time healing, laying in the sun, laughing, getting hit on by seventy-something-year-old men trying to buy me drinks, reading books, visiting Disney World, napping, and renting a luxury condo for the week. It was one of the dreamiest vacations I've ever been on. The best part, I got to be my authentic self. I didn't have to concern myself with what others thought of me, or if they were upset I may have been in the same city as them. I got to be myself doing what I wanted to for the first time in over 14.5 years. It was nice not having to fulfill a false narrative or do what someone else wanted me to.

Don't get me wrong, there were ex-family members who were irate I was there, and one of the hotels I stayed in was swamped with cheerleaders, so I asked if Piper and Zoe were there, but I didn't know this one question was going to send them off their rockers. I mean I asked Xavier who was supposed to go with me, but he changed his mind. He's the one who said something to them. I'm guessing he likes drama a little more than he let on.

You know, if you lose your ish because someone asked a question, in my opinion, you need serious help. There's no shame in getting help, and my extended ex-family could use some.

I put myself first, and that was the sexiest thing about this vacation. So what if I asked a question? I was curious. Besides, these two that flipped their ish encouraged me to be myself. So, what if they don't like it now that I'm my real self?

As for the rest of the vacation, it was fantastic. I even saw Goofy stopping for a few photo ops on my way to ride the new Star Wars excursion. I don't remember what it was called but if you're in the area, I highly suggest you experience it. It's not just for Star Wars enthusiasts.

Momma's had enough

Let's rewind to December 2022; actually, let's go to the fall football season of 2022. At this point, I was still welcome to attend my kid's games. Xavier was playing football for the varsity football team, and the girls were cheering. It was exciting watching them all participate at the same time. Piper was a flier for her squad, and Zoe was a base. She also did some pretty wild flips. I'm not sure how either of them stays balanced, but they're pretty cool to watch.

It was nice having our "family" together. It's actually more like being on *the Jerry Springer* show with everything that has occurred, but that's my life. I can only control myself. At times, we can all get along; then there are other times Karen is losing her stuff trying to boss everyone around because she has a false narrative to fulfill.

It was actually kinda funny. I was sitting with Karen and her friend Ronnie. These two were complimenting each other on their "Cheer Mom" shirts, and Ronnie noticed I didn't have one. She told me they should get me a shirt. Haha, and then there was silence and a grimaced look on Karen's face. I just laughed and said I appreciated the thought, but I didn't want a shirt. Karen always had to be the "cheer mom," and that's okay. I know who I am. I'm a badass stepmom who shows up. I have that T-shirt.

It was nice of her to include me, but the validation Karen needs being a "cheer mom" wasn't worth it. She's the mom that has to be the know-it-all and pretend like everyone wants to be her. She even wore this heated jacket she had to keep showing off. Like good for you! Are you getting paid for your networking and marketing at this football game? Oh, wait, I forgot you don't like network marketing of any kind. What was I thinking?

So anywho, now you have a glimpse of how it was inside my "family." It was great for me to be there but never seen. I never felt like a part of the family, no matter how much effort I put forth. I felt like the invisible woman. The invisible step-momma working behind the scenes. I was the one who had a heavy workload with no help. So yes, when you live like I have for years, never being seen and suicidal at times, you're going to get angry. You're going to tell people to F off when they're nosey enough to stalk you on your social media and criticize you but don't show up in your life. Sometimes I just have to be the F-bomb mom. Next time, don't poke the bear.

I was the one you ran to when your mom embarrassed you or got on your nerves. When she stepped on your toes and didn't consider your feelings, you ran to me. It's time to grow up. If you're upset with her or anyone else for that matter, you need to go directly to them. Stop hiding behind triangle conversations and reckless behavior. Stop hurting your own feelings by creating new social media accounts so you can see accounts you've been blocked from because you can't handle it and you're trying to control other people. Try meeting people where they are.

23

DYNAMITE

I did it.

I blew the heck out of everything.

Roughly two years ago, my life was blown to smithereens. I decided I was going to give my haters a show. I did exactly as they told me not to. I don't know who they think they are, but I'm not scared of them anymore. I got my power back, baby!

Ya know, kinda like when Jesus died and His haters thought, *Good, the problem is dead and taken care of.* Then three days later, He blew that rock away like dynamite. Well, this is how I imagine Him rising from the dead. I bet He would have had some cool music playing, His hair blowing in the wind as He ascended into Heaven, maybe some cool dance moves, and the look on God's face as His son came home. Maybe God danced with Him too. Man, I bet that was a memorable moment. Every Easter, the Resurrection blows my mind. Jesus is like dynamite to me. Boom, there He is! Whoop! Whoop!

I know I just dated myself, but I don't care. Show me those dance moves! Shake it! Let your happiness find you.

As I was saying, the unbelievable forgiveness and grace He gives to each of us moves me. It moves me in ways you couldn't imagine. My Jesus is BIG, and He has truly been my rock.

I did it. I did exactly as He commanded me. I got scared when I was writing this book. Putting everything out there shakes me. I feel like I'm naked and exposed, and God moves me to be the person He wants me to be. When I didn't write, I would develop this insane amount of anxiety I couldn't function. I would physically shake. Then when I wrote, every anxiety pent up inside of me would fade away.

I knew it was God's will for me to write this book. He's the one who put it in my soul. He's the one who held the pen all these years as I grew and changed throughout the years. My story is His story. He's the Father who has always loved me. He has always chosen me, and, with tears in my eyes, I can finally say I have wholeheartedly chosen Him.

I finally trust Him to hold the pen in His hand. I may not agree with the story He's writing, but I do trust Him. I trust Him with every fiber of my being that He carefully stitched together. You see, I recently found a picture of me on my sixth birthday. I was so proud of this cheeseburger cake my grandmother Alice had brought over and held it with such pride. This little girl was going to change the world. She was going to move mountains and shake things up. She was the strong-willed one who would chase every moment and take every chance presented to her.

Her blue eyes shined as she took on the world. She was going to be the difference maker. Then life happened.

The other side

She started seeing the unfortunate side of life. The side that can swallow you whole. She decided instead of wearing a smile, it would be better to wear a rock-like expression. She noticed if you have a harder face, people won't hurt you as much. I had to protect myself, so I hid my smile for those rare and special moments.

I felt like I had to be responsible for everyone else. I felt like I had to walk around with the weight of the world on my shoulders, even as a little kid. Some days, this is the reason I feel like Mara and I have more in common than we'd like to admit. I think she has had to walk around with the weight of the world on her shoulders too.

Mara

Being the oldest sibling in our family wasn't always easy, especially since she functions like a "Little Mommy" when she would bark orders at me. She really didn't appreciate it when I did not listen to her. If her mom wasn't around, then she was expected to be the "mom." I didn't let this slide in my house. I had more respect for her childhood than the other adults in our family.

Mara was constantly trying to boss me around and run my house so from my perspective, she had a heavy load to carry around as a kid. I think it colored her world as an adult and not in a positive way. I wish the other adults in her life would have handled the weight instead of making a kid carry it around.

Changes

Watching her grow through the years, I watched the smile fade from her face. She used to be this kid who would dance around with her sisters, Piper and Zoe, in my front room. They would wear tutus and scarfs while putting on dances for us. They would use the room divider and pop out from behind it, just like they did when they were putting on a dance recital with their teams or when they performed in competitions. Dance competitions are insane! One time, the girls had to be there at four or so in the morning. These were little kids having to be at a competition, and their parents were barely making it. We brought four cups of coffee to wake everyone up. If I recall the kids' reactions after that, it was kinda like when Alvin and the Chipmunks had coffee. They were funny to watch.

So, you see, all of them had a lot on their shoulders. I always tried to make it better, even when Xavier would come to their dance competitions. I felt sorry for the poor kid. It was nice he was there to support his sisters, but Karen never wanted to be his stepmother and never was. She's the girls' mom, and she tried to control what he did when he was there along, with JJ and myself.

She would change the rules like there was food allowed in the auditorium at one competition, and the next competition you couldn't have food, so when I tried to keep the peace by putting his food in my purse, she would start drama by calling his mom. She didn't know what was going on and never had the common sense to ask. She wasn't his mom and should have stayed in her own lane but asking her to do that was impossible because she's a know-it-all. She always assumed everything and acted like she was royalty because she was a "dance mom," and he had nothing to do with dance. Barf!

When she saw me being a mother to him, she would get jealous and cause problems. This made extracurricular activities a little stressful because she was starting drama, and she didn't want Xavier around the girls, let alone us. If you want to see a mom on a power trip, go find Karen. Her behavior is laughable some days. She yelled at me for using a bathroom Mara showed me because "it was too close to the dressing room." Mara was confused and so was I. This was the only bathroom available to me yet she's screaming I cannot use it. I guess she would have preferred me to pee on the floor. I guess this would have been more acceptable since I was just a "stepmother." This seems reasonable especially since we were standing in the middle of a Christian Church. She always has to make everything about her and if you don't play by her rules, watch out.

Stepmom

This is what my life was like as a stepmom with four children and two moms at odds. I often got stuck in the middle because JJ cheated on them too. It was hard raising my kids because their moms were at odds with each other, so this meant the kids were at odds with each other. To give you an idea, when the kids arrived on Fridays, they would draw ugly pictures of each other's moms, and they would say cruel things about them. This got so bad some days I had to take the pictures and trash them. These kids were stuck in the middle, and it wasn't fair, but I was right there with them. Somedays it felt like we were growing up together.

Game plan

As a stepmom, I had to be three steps ahead of everyone. To me, this means I had to have everything set up and ready to go before the kids came over. I had to have groceries bought for the most part, except for the treats the kids wanted to get. I also had to have my weekends planned in advance.

I also always had to look over my shoulder. I had to be on alert all the time. Going through abuse with JJ and being bullied by the bio-moms was no easy feat. Heck, my kids bullied me too. I guess at least when the kids were doing it, they were mimicking what they saw their parents do.

Karen would tell me she never encouraged the girls to be mean to me, but I highly doubt that. When they smashed my makeup and went home, they didn't get in trouble. I'm guessing she thought it was funny they were mean to me. They liked stealing my things, and JJ never replaced them. They also hit and grabbed me and never had any consequences from my spouse. The kids were learning from their parents how to talk to and treat me. Meanwhile, I was fighting to keep my house rules intact, including the kids not smoking or bringing vapes into the house while they were underage, but their dad was vaping and purchasing them vape juice illegally so why would they listen to me?

If you're being abused or have been abused and you're raising step-kids who are stuck in the middle, they may be mimicking what they've seen. They want to stay on their parents' good side and don't want to upset them or, worse, get in trouble for loving a stepparent, I mean unless it's a step-dad who swooped in and "saved" the day, you can love him but how dare you love your stepmother? How dare you be nice to her when she's nice to you?

This was my position for many years, seeing as JJ and I were "a packaged deal." I didn't treat everyone else like crap, but it was "fair" in their eyes for them to treat me like crap. They made me pay for his sins. This is why the Resurrection is so incredibly important to me. Jesus could have quit if He didn't listen to God's will. He could have just stayed dead and never got up, but He didn't.

Jesus encourages me to be strong when I don't want to be and by His example, by His Resurrection, I'm free and so are you. This is what busting out of my marriage was like. It was like when Jesus blew that rock off the tomb and rose from the dead. When I was married, my real self died. I didn't get to be who I was supposed to be, but now that I've been set free from his sins, I get to be me. I also won't be turning a blind eye when people treat me like crap. I'll be telling them how it is when I stand up for myself. I would encourage you too, with tact.

PHOENIX RISING

24

IMAGINE

Imagine being the woman who looked at the love of her life because she was extremely thankful that she was yours and you were hers.

Think about that smile that crossed her face every time you walked into the room. The way she admired the curve of your smile or the arch from your derriere. The way she got off the couch to unlock the door and wait for you to enter your home. The way she gave you one hundred percent of her attention when you graced the room with your presence. The way she greeted you showed the value she afforded you.

The way she would wait on you showed how much she missed you throughout the day because you wouldn't return her texts. After all, you claimed to be too "busy" for your wife, and now she stood in lingerie with her makeup done for you. The only thing you said to her was … "I'm not in the mood tonight."

You may have not considered it but the woman standing vulnerable and open to you, the one being so thankful that she was yours, just had her spirit irreversibly crushed. Never again would she put herself out there, waiting for you to come home and make love to her. Never again would she want your body on top of hers. You undid everything you built together in one moment. Actually, many moments, but this blow was the most devastating.

The woman who thanked God for the day she met you was demolished.

The way she looked at you was gone. She realized everything she had imagined about you reflected herself. She thought you were the one who had a heart of gold. She thought you wanted what was best for those around you. But she was wrong.

The instances she was thankful for every moment she spent with you were gone. The songs you listened to in your black, two-door-Jeep Wrangler Sport were suddenly erased. Those magical moments were obliterated. Her imagination was no longer running wild. She no longer waited for the moment she was washing dishes in lingerie and waited for you to place your pulsating member on her and take her. You'd press your lips against her skin, telling her how she was the only one for you. The daydreams she dreamt were gone. The lingerie was no longer sexy. She shredded each piece with distaste and threw it in the trash.

She was bold and tenacious. She held onto every dream and promise as though it would come true. She had been hurt before, and she trusted you. Her whole soul and body are on display for you to ravage. The trust she gave you was one she had never given anyone before, and now it was all gone. This woman who once loved the life she had did not recognize the man standing in front of her.

Was he even a man? What man would build a woman so high just to tear her down? What man would reject a woman like this? A woman who had invested so much time into this man. She did everything she could to make him feel wanted, valued, worthy, successful and acknowledged. She took so much time out of her life noticing him that she forgot herself.

Who is she?

Yes, in the midst of my life, I forgot who I was before I met and married JJ. I forgot the woman I was placed here to be. I forgot everything about myself. I even forgot how to have fun and see the world as a child. The jaded woman I had become was not me. I no longer wanted to be the woman who looked into the mirror and did not recognize the reflection looking back at me.

When I was eighteen years old, just finishing my senior year of high school, I had the whole world at my fingertips. I was going to change the world. I was going to make it a better place. I was going to be the one who made other people feel seen. I was going to make sure they felt valued.

I did that and accomplished what I set out to do. Each time Mara, Xavier, Piper, and Zoe entered their last year of high school, it forced me to reminisce. It made me remember the girl I was at that time in my life.

That girl I had long forgotten. The girl who was so intensely focused on making other people happy, that she forgot she had an opinion. She worked so hard for the approval of others, that she lost sight of what this world had to offer.

Rediscovery of myself

As I hit the age of thirty-seven, my world was shattered. All the tears I cried on my couch finally filled up the hourglass. I imagine it bursting and flooding the waiting room in Heaven. The flood was so colossal, God could no longer let it go. I am guessing it was like a hurricane overwhelming the room. When God held each of my tears in His hand, He felt my pain. My Father saw His daughter asking for His help. "Daddy, please help me" is what crossed my mind. "When are you going to help me, Daddy? When are you going to step in as my protector? I thought you loved me no matter what."

At this moment, I imagine my heavenly Daddy crying with me. His thinking that I didn't feel loved and alone probably was an awful pain for Him to experience. He had to do something. My daddy had seen me cry for far too many years, and when He stood and said enough is enough, the storm that came through my life was a tsunami.

He sent a storm into my life and when it was finished, my life was unrecognizable. Everything around me was completely shattered. My life was changed in an instant. Everything I once held in my hand no longer had meaning. Where love once lived, there was only excruciating pain.

The aftermath

My daddy did it. He ruined my life for good. He looked at his thirty-seven-year-old daughter, knowing if He did not ruin her life, it was going to ruin her. He knew the miracle she was praying desperately for was never coming because it did not align with His will.

He created this daughter of His with a tenacious, fiery spirit to hold on and withstand the hard times. This time was not it. She had learned her lesson, and the only way for her to be set free was for Him to reset her life.

It was time for her to let everything go. Everything she had collected and kept in her heart over the last thirty-seven years was time to let it all go.

She always thought she had to be a good role model, momma, step-momma, wife, daughter, sister, friend, and teacher. Whatever label she came up with, she had to let it all go to rediscover who she really is.

The aftermath that came from my daddy destroying my life helped me connect with Him on a deeper level and to myself. To my real self. Yes, I prayed and read scripture nightly, but He needed to get me into a place where I only depended on Him.

My daddy did not want to hold only my tears in His hands, He wanted to hold me, and He wanted to make certain I found myself.

Recreating my life

He did it again. My daddy stepped up to the plate and showed me how BIG He is. He not only sent a storm to destroy what He hated, but He used His love to recreate what had been lost.

You see, in 2017, I thought I could give everything up just like my mentor. She left a huge house in the mountains with her own personal tennis and basketball courts for a cookie-cutter house in the suburbs. I glanced around my house and thought the same. I did not have the wealth she did, but I still gave up everything He gave to me.

It's true. I sold my house and moved into a small bedroom. The only things I kept can fit in this room. I didn't rent a storage unit or borrow someone's garage. I sold, donated, or trashed everything I couldn't take with me.

God planted this seed in my heart in 2017, and it came to fruition, fully, in January 2022. He helped me sell everything I owned. He even sent me two buyers for my house before it was on the market. He also sent a sweet woman to my garage sale who contacted her friend to tell her husband to come check out all my stuff. I loved meeting this older man. In all the chaos, he brought me a little joy.

I mean it was the beginning of December in 2022, and I was holding a garage sale with zero signs, and this guy showed up to buy the majority of my stuff. I asked God to send people to my garage sale, and He did. He showed off so much, He sent people to come haul away the stuff I didn't sell.

I want to put this into perspective so to top it off, I didn't have money to pay my mortgage. I was so stressed out, I had been upset and my hair was falling out. My mortgage was due in four days, and I had no way to pay it.

I was also still supporting my stepchildren at this point. If they called me up, I would purchase whatever I could to help them. I even saved money to pay for Xavier's letterman jacket, emoji cleats, and gloves for football. Plus, I had forced time off from work due to the Thanksgiving holiday, and school was out for the week. I only got to work when my students were in school. This meant no school, no paycheck.

God showed up big! He sold my house, most of the stuff at my garage sale, found people to haul off what didn't sell, and helped me provide for my children. I don't know about you, but I needed Him to show up big. I needed Him to be the man in my life.

I'm guessing if you learn how to lean on Him, He will show up big for you too. He could possibly change your life too if you let Him. It's up to you to allow Him to recreate your life, just like He did mine.

You just gotta give him the reigns and sit back to follow His lead.

It's hard to do, but it's definitely doable.

And the best part is ... He's not done yet.

25

NEW BEGINNINGS

This is where my story takes a turn for the better. He stayed silent for too long. He attempted to remain unscathed and on top of the world, but I noticed. I saw right through him. Who needs to sit on the toilet for forty-five minutes at a time taking a dump? I knew what he was doing. I'm an over-thinker. I've always been an over-thinker, ever since I was little. I know when something doesn't feel right, or something is off. He coached me not to say anything so I didn't. I continued to play stupid while I stayed vigilant, taking mental notes.

I took notes as to why the kids were no longer coming every other weekend when he claimed he was a committed father. He said he wouldn't let a weekend go by with his "B**** of an ex-wife" to keeping the children away. He knew he must do something so he was taking her to court. Yea, right. I thought this was more of a show for him to prove how awesome he was in front of the judge. He was so amazing at manipulation that he didn't want me there so I didn't expose his garbage and his lies so I allowed it. You see, he didn't realize when he spoke, he was telling me his truths. I knew the kids were becoming too much for him to handle. They were all growing into fine young people, and I told them this often. They became a competition for him. My eyes were not solely on him anymore. He didn't get to be the father who looked squeaky clean anymore. He became the enemy because I loved the children.

These children he brought into my life and me into theirs. He praised me for being a "good mom to them and a wonderful wife" until I stopped playing his games. That's when I became a bad mother and wife. I didn't give into every minuscule desire he had. I fought with him! I demanded to know why our children were not coming over. Why were they missing another visit? Why isn't he standing up to do something about it? Why is he sitting in his chair, watching television or messing with his phone rather than making sure we are getting the most out of these last precious years with our children? Why?

Every time I questioned him, he would look at me with a sullen, empty look and tell me to leave it alone. He commanded me like I was a dog who should be corrected. I was something to be ruled not listened to, or so he thought. This made me fill up with a lot of attitude and made me wonder why. It made me think deeper and wonder what was going on in his head just to let the kids go. At this time, our son had stopped staying over for about three years, my eldest daughter stopped for about five years, and our twin daughters only came when they could make it work. It seemed to me like they were putting all the effort in to earn my ex's approval rather than him stepping up to be the father that should have been seeking them out. They had to beg to come over, but they only got to stay for about twenty-four hours or less. The reality I was living in was weird. I didn't like it, but I didn't know how to get out. I knew I could only change me, and I was no longer wasting my time on changing him. I gave him back to God. I didn't want anything from him anymore.

Fast forward to the last time they came over; it was late February 2021. Actually, it was my niece's birthday. I wanted to go celebrate with her, but I was told that the kids had requested my presence on this trip. That actually turned out to be another lie, but I assume it was because he wanted me to go on one more family trip without him having to ask. It was another way for him to control me without him being caught.

We drove to the University of Notre Dame. This is a trip my ex had been promising to take our kids on since they were in elementary school, and now they were all upperclassmen in high school except for our eldest daughter, who's a grown adult.

Notre Dame is one of those places that I will always hold dear. It has everything to do with me being an Irish Catholic, and I'm proud of that. It's nice to have roots, and the presence on this campus is seriously cool. My childhood hero, Rudy, attended college here. I knew I was different growing up with a learning disability, but it wasn't so bad with a hero like him showing me I could do anything I wanted to in my life; so in a way, this place will always be a second home to me.

So anyways, we spent the day walking around the campus, talking about the kids' futures with them, shopping in the big bookstore for hours, and grabbing some lunch. It was a nice break for me to get to do something with my family, even though there was still something really off about the trip. I noticed that my ex had wanted to take pictures with the kids, but he wasn't taking any with me. Touchdown Jesus is a popular picture you will see many visitors snap a picture of but when I tried to get in the family photo, I was scoffed at by my ex.

Later that day, I asked for my picture to be taken in front of the Kelly School of Business where I was met with groans and comments to hurry up. Yet, "Prince Charming" was able to take his sweet time doing whatever he wanted, and I had to be rushed along.

We stopped at the Grotto, lit a candle, and prayed. I had been begging God for a way for us to repair our marriage, and I thought this was the moment it was going to happen. I had been wanting a stronger connection with my then-husband. I thought maybe, just maybe, this was the moment God was going to use to change his heart. The moment we both knelt down to pray seemed powerful to me. It seemed like time stood still while we both prayed publicly in front of our children. It was a powerful moment for me. When we stood up, made the sign of the cross, and walked away, it was like a show.

I wondered again who I was married to. Who is this person that is talking to our kids right now? It didn't seem like their father but some person trying to collect points for praying. It felt like a real-life Mario collecting points for hitting the box of coins in the video game. That's not what prayer was about, and I was hoping it helped the kids to see me pray because I meant it.

I don't remember what I prayed that day, but I remember feeling at peace when I stood up. I remember wanting and seeking a deeper relationship with my Lord. I remembered wanting to set a good example for three teenagers who are susceptible to this world and its practices. I know I want to raise children to be better than I ever have. I want them to be happy, healthy, and know that they are loved beyond measure. At this point in my life, I've stuck around to make sure those exact things happen. I stayed this long to make sure they are taken care of because I've felt like that's the only reason I married into this family, to care for them.

After this, we drove the kids home so they could get back to their lives, and we got back to ours. I've never liked the end of a visit where we go our separate ways, but that's life. My ex didn't really talk to me, and once again I was alone. The silence was deafening, but I could hear more clearly. I could hear everything that wasn't being said.

In July of 2020, I begged God to reveal to me what was going on. I needed to know what was going on behind the scenes that I couldn't see. I wanted to know, no matter the consequences. I needed to be free. The weight on my shoulders was too heavy. I wanted nothing more than to put it down and move on. I was tired of being the one with all the responsibilities in life while my ex went around town with his flirtatious attitude with what seemed like everything was at his fingertips ... all he had to do was bat his eyes and tell a few lies, and he would get whatever he wanted. He went on a "guys trip" on our tenth wedding anniversary, and then suddenly those trips started becoming more frequent. I didn't care because I had given him back to God in March of that year. I had a choice to make. I had to choose him, or I had to choose me; those were my only options. One option would keep me trapped, wondering what I did wrong to deserve all the pain that was coming my way and the other choice set me free. I chose me. I chose FREEDOM. I chose to reignite the fire in my soul and be the woman God sent me here to be.

I didn't realize it then, but I had been plugging into personal development between multiple coaches, and I could no longer stay stagnant. I started reaching out more. The training I had learned and studied took over. I had even purchased pieces of training a year before that addressed me as a spiritual person that I didn't know I needed, but suddenly, they seemed to hit home. I started seeking God's real voice. It wasn't His audible voice, but it was more of a feeling of conviction. One of my coaches taught me to feel in my being if I vibed with something or not. This opened a spiritual can of whoop-ass if you know what I mean. Yea, you probably wouldn't imagine a spiritual can of ass, but this woman knows how to serve it up. She did for reals. She made me realize I was out here playing small when I was sent here to play in the big leagues. She is the real deal, and she reawakened me. I'll be forever grateful for her enlightenment.

I took her pieces of training and all the other training and combined them. At this point, I started hearing how my ex "hated" so-and-so. How he couldn't stand this or that. I thought maybe I wasn't listening to the training the right way, so I backed off. I tried to understand his perspective. However, what I came to realize was that his hatred of these training programs was because I was becoming a stronger woman. I was learning to put boundaries into place, and I cut him off financially.

When you have been enabling someone with money because you thought it was helping them and you cut them off, it tends to annoy them. Instead of pouring all my extra money into my ex, I started putting all my money into more training and paying off debt. Life sucks when you're buried alive under debt. You can't breathe, and you want life to get better, so you must apply what you learned and take action.

I picked me. I decided I wanted to be free and use every training I had listened to, to become the best person I could be. I wanted time freedom, debt freedom, and mostly I wanted the opportunity to see the world, since I had been a slave to my mortgage and other bills for so long. I was the main provider in the house, but now it was time for that to change. I was tired of working like a dog for little pay.

It was time for growth. It was time for me to endure the same test I had been given by God for many years. It was time for me to prove that my boundaries were firmly in place. The last big purchase I was allowing my ex to use was to buy the family Jeep. It was to be his Jeep, but I say family because it has my name on it. His credit was so bad because he refused to pay his bills; my credit is the only one he could rely on. He even put three red marks on my credit report because he defaulted on car payments he was supposed to be making. Instead, he would lie to me and say he was looking for a different car instead of taking the responsibility of paying the bills.

He didn't care when my credit took a hit, but I stopped funding his stupidity. He tested me often on this boundary, told me that he was trying to get financed for a four-door Jeep, but it never happened.

Then when our eldest daughter mentioned she was looking into college, I told him I was not going to finance her education since I had financed a majority of the things she needed growing up. When I said this wasn't my responsibility, he stopped speaking to me like I knew he would. He apparently burnt so many bridges with her that we didn't get an invite to her high school graduation. He refused to give her $500 so she could further her education after high school at a dental school, but he wouldn't do it. I later offered to pay half, and he still wouldn't do it because she didn't play by his "rules" either. We were two women who failed to follow his "rules," and there was no way we were stopping now.

Instead of going to her high school graduation and cheering her on from the parking lot, like I wanted, he took me to a camper lot to show me a teardrop camper. I was curious as to what they were, but that's all I was interested in. I wasn't particularly happy that this is what we were going to do while Mara was taking her first adult steps into the world. Shopping for a camper was the last thing I wanted to be doing. I did get to see her graduate on the live stream that was delayed, and a glitch caused me to miss her walking across the stage. Insert the ugliest angry face a woman could sport. Yup, that's what my face looked like. That was me.

Who wouldn't want to go shopping for a camper with that expression on their face? I tried to make the best of my time. I played along and tried to be a good sport until I was sitting in the finance office, and I was told the finance guy "needed" to run my numbers.

Hold on! I only asked out of curiosity what a camper like this would cost. I asked for a rough number and told the guys I was only interested in paying cash for any new toys, especially one like this that I didn't want and was not interested in paying for. You see, my ex never paid the back taxes he owed to the Internal Revenue Service (IRS), and I knew as soon as I signed for this sucker and it hit my credit report, they were going to come get it. I knew this because I had a lengthy conversation with them since my ex refused to pay his bill.

He must have thought I would be dumb enough to let him run my numbers after I had already told him I was never financing anything for him again. Apparently, he didn't believe me until I went toe-to-toe with him in the finance office, and we didn't leave with his precious camper that he wanted to use to impress the woman in the state of Wisconsin whom he had been having an affair with. She informed me that he talked a really big game that he was going to buy this camper and bring it back the next weekend, except that he couldn't bring it up because he hadn't bought it yet. My not financing his pipe dream really threw a wrench in his plans. It was then that her best friend started asking questions but thank God the Holy Spirit had already been dropping me hints and talking to me for a long time.

My ex didn't stop there. He continued to play nice and drive me around to different camper stores until one day I told him it was never going to happen. I was never going to buy a camper for him or me, and he needed to step up and help me get serious about the debt we already had. He refused, screaming at me like a toddler having a temper tantrum. It was so bad that his entire face turned beat red. There was no way I was backing down. I knew this guy was muscular and most likely would have put my entire body through a wall, but I wasn't backing down. Nope, not today Satan. I kept pressing him to the point he took our dogs and slept in my daughters' room. I knew at this point he wasn't coming out, and I was most likely the one that was going to have to take charge of all the finances permanently.

What you need to understand was, at this time, he had been abusing me for years. My trauma bonded me to him, and he never thought I'd get away. I even went to the extent of letting him know that my credit cards were maxed out. That made him happy, not. I had actually started paying off my credit cards, but I kept them locked at all times. I only unlocked them when I needed something, and my paychecks wouldn't cover it. I got a good kick out of this. Let's be real though; if you won't help finance our daughter's future with $500 but you think I'm going to finance, at a minimum, a $15,000 camper that you don't need, you are outside of your mind. How selfish do you have to be to trash your daughter's future but want me to buy you a camper so you can impress your every-other-weekend affair partner?

No, it's time things changed. This is where my new beginning starts.

26

THE COMEBACK

In my early thirties, I was unforgiving. At times, it felt like it was me against the world. I didn't feel as though I could trust anyone. It's the world I was living in. Maybe you can relate; I felt this way to a fault. I can't believe I'm telling you this because it's so embarrassing, but I couldn't even trust God. Yea, how do you like that for humble pie?

I didn't trust the Father who created me and sent me here to fulfill His purpose. As far as I knew, I had Him figured out. In my mind, He was an old guy with a long white beard, writing every wrong I committed. He was just waiting for me to die so He could read my laundry list of wrongs I did throughout my entire life.

I don't know about you, but this was my problem. The perspective in which I viewed God. I decided He was a mean, old nasty man waiting to throw me in Hell. I kinda figured this might be why I ended up in a marriage where my prayers were not being answered. He was punishing me now instead of waiting for me to die.

The truth is, I was judging God from my view. I could only see what was right in front of me. I couldn't see what He saw for me. He created me from the end of my life to the beginning. He already knew the move I was going to make. He knew it, and He still chose me. He chose me just like He chose you. I've learned He's a loving Father who puts us in situations to bring us closer to Him.

You don't have to agree with me, and I hope you won't dismiss me for what or who I believe in. The year my marriage crumbled, I had placed all my faith in someone who didn't deserve that kind of trust. He wasn't built for that level of honor.

I kept feeling as though I should put on a warrior's suit of armor. I didn't know what this meant, and it seemed like every time I turned around or scrolled on social media, there was a woman dressed in armor. This was a woman prepared for battle. Her war paint was carefully applied, her armor carefully tightened, and her facial expression was confident and intense. This woman knew her purpose, and I knew I wanted to be like her. Maybe you've even felt this way before something monumental happened.

You didn't know what was coming, but you knew it was coming. You could feel the vibrations in your spirit. You could feel the energy all around you. This is your moment! This is your time to shine. It's time for your comeback!

I don't know what your comeback looks like, but mine has removed me from everything I knew. I quit my job I'd been working for ten years, earned a position I've been dreaming about since I was ten years old, and decided to express myself through a photo shoot that included boxing gloves. Yea, I'm designing a life I love! And this woman I'm becoming ... I freaking LOVE her!

I decided no matter what hit came at me, I was getting back up. In my kickboxing class, I learned you must be swift and strike fast. This is how I see myself now. The world might have gotten some good punches in and knocked me to the floor, but I'm not staying there. I put on a dress, strapped on my boxing gloves, and looked at the camera with my war paint on.

My armor isn't the same as the warrior women I looked at. NOPE, this is my armor. This life is mine, and I can choose what I want to wear and who I want to be. The same is true for you, friend.

You can choose who you want to be in this world. My abuser

might have been dictating to me what and whom he needed me to be, but not anymore. That chapter is gone.

This is the new chapter of life where you get to get back up and kick butt. You get to throw punches at the things and people who wanted you to fail. They won't know what hit them when they see you succeed. They will think they know exactly who you are, but they don't.

They won't know you because the woman they hit and left crying on the floor is completely different now. You're a new breed of woman. You're reconstructed, steady, confident, and swift. They won't be able to hit you because you'll see it coming a hundred miles away.

Your battle plan will be locked and loaded. You almost want them to throw a punch so you can walk away. Your strength will cause them insurmountable damage. Imagine showing them your shiny new shield of confidence.

THIS IS YOUR TIME!

GET UP!

You are UNSTOPPABLE!

Welcome to your comeback; it's time to fight the good fight.

27

REMINDERS

Moving into this next season of life, I want you to remember some good points as you courageously press on.

The adventure may have been challenging and the worst time in your life, but it was, in fact, worth it. The person you are today and have the chance to become is possible.

I know it might seem scary to walk into a room all by yourself but know this; I've been walking through the ugliest and most beautiful seasons of my life. The woman I am now would not be writing this book had I missed out on the experiences God allowed to slip through His fingers. The experiences He knew I needed in order to shape me into the woman He needed me to become.

It's true, my friend. He chose me for this pain. I used to loathe walking into a room by myself. I'd have to give myself a pep talk, turn on high-vibing music, and focus on the moment. I'd remind myself I can do hard things. I still broke out into a sweat because I was so nervous, but I did it. I was the woman who couldn't stand what people would think or who I would talk to. I always felt so rushed to find someone I knew. I had to strike up a conversation with the first person I saw with the most profound sigh of relief. I lacked the confidence to walk around the room by myself; thankfully I'm much more confident than I used to be.

I even did this same routine when I went to see Mara, Xavier, Piper, and Zoe at their school events. I didn't know my worth; therefore, Karen would harass me when I came to their events. She's not a mother to all of them, and I was told she refused to be a stepmother to Xavier so she behaved as though she could tell me what to do, no matter what child it was.

The old me would falter because I received so many mixed messages. Haha, but the badass woman I am today has the gumption to stand up for herself. Karen can no longer tell me what to do, and that's pretty freaking amazing.

This new version of me owns my worth when I walk into a room, auditorium, stadium, or gymnasium. I'm the good stuff. Seriously, I wish I could look you in the eyes and give you a hug because you're the good stuff too. It's okay to know you are the good stuff and don't shy away from it. Shout it from the rooftops of your heart! This is the way my heavenly Father created me to be, and I'm guessing if you looked deep within yourself, you'll find it too.

Always remember, it's a good day to take a chance and believe in yourself. I'm worth it and so are you. I also want you to remember this: we are not made for perfection; it doesn't exist. Being real ... that does. You taking a chance on yourself, that's something worth doing. Take time and rediscover who you are.

I dare you to eat at a restaurant alone, leaving your phone in your pocket and soaking up every second of your newfound independence. Relearn who you are now and heal so that the little kid whose hurt deep within your soul can have a chance to see the world through a new lens. Be the hero she always needed.

Be the you that you actually would like to be. Take a hold of the pen along with God and start writing. It's a game-changer when you start writing with Him. When you start checking in with God on every part of your life, life changes. He wants you to have the BEST life possible. This is your chance to be a co-author with Him. Don't be afraid to write a new chapter because your life is waiting on you.

And lastly, be audacious and celebrate the wins in your life. You've made it this far, and every part of your life from here on out deserves a celebration. I know it's nice to celebrate with others but be empowered enough to celebrate yourself the way you would want someone else to celebrate you. The way you have celebrated others.

Baby girl, you are worth it. Every tear, every moment, every birthday, every Mother's Day, every Christmas, every Thanksgiving, every second someone else didn't celebrate you, it's your turn. Celebrate yourself! See yourself. Validate yourself. BE yourself ... because with you, this world is brighter.

28

REALIZATION

The moment of realization hit me like two cars violently smashing into each other. You know the kind when someone blew through a bloody red traffic light. The catastrophic sound you can hear from blocks away when the crash happens. That's precisely what this moment felt like.

JJ and I had been separated for fifteen and a half months at this time. We were legally divorced, and my healing had taken me to a place of realization. I know some of you may have had the same experience as I have had and some may have not, but the realization that struck me was that JJ will never change. I can change, but he lacks the ability to change. He doesn't have the capacity for it.

I can reflect, analyze, and identify where I need to improve. I can confidently improve myself as life progresses, but JJ cannot. I've observed him through the years, and I have noticed patterns. I have worked with little kids for more than a decade and within this time, I have noticed patterns with these children as they grow up. They might advance from grade to grade, but their behavior stays the same. Some children ultimately learn how to manage their choices whereas some don't.

JJ was the latter of these children. I know this might sound silly, analyzing my ex-husband in this way, but I can confidently say no one has ever loved him as much as I did. No one has ever spent the amount of time trying to understand him the way I did, some days still do. I have spent a great deal of time over the last decade picking apart our relationship to understand what I did wrong. I'm guessing you may have done the same things during or after your relationship; however, I realized it was not me.

Yes!

I said what I said.

It was not me.

I am the one who can reflect and improve myself ... he cannot.

I was sitting on the soft, comfy couch in my counselor's office when I had this revelation.

JJ cannot change ... this hit me like a brick wall.

I wondered when he was going to experience punishment for putting everyone through pain. I was not only thinking about myself but everyone in our family. I was thinking about every single person he had tormented with his choices. The times he failed to pick our children up for visitation. He had the audacity to get mad at me because I wanted to pick them up when he wouldn't.

The times he chose not to show up to their school events. The moments they needed and wanted him, and he had the nerve not to show up. The times he told me I couldn't go to their events because he didn't want to, and it would make him look bad, or he didn't want their mothers calling and inquiring why I was there and he wasn't. Uggh! When was justice going to be served? When was he going to pay? In this brief moment, I realized he had already been paying.

JJ was already serving a life sentence. He can never change. He is imprisoned in his physical body and mind. He has even lost his spirit. He has no idea who he is. That is so sad! It is sad to live in this world and not know who you are. How sad it is he will not get to know the person he was sent here to be. He's trapped in a shell of a person. A person who mimics a chameleon changing colors, except instead of changing colors, he changes his personality and interests with every person he meets. He mirrors every person he encounters so he can gain attention from them.

I know this is what he is doing. I have watched him. He did this with me at the beginning of our relationship. His son, Xavier, was not in the picture when we started dating, and I commented, "I won't date a deadbeat dad. I will only date a man who takes care of his children and pays his child support. If he does not do this, then I don't want to be a part of his life." In a split second, he explained how important his children were to him. He said he took the best care of his kids. I later discovered this was not true.

Xavier only started coming around because I entered the picture. I find it repulsive that this is the only reason he got invited to be in our lives. Don't get me wrong; I love Xavier, and I'm incredibly thankful to have him for my son, but knowing his father was blaming his mother as to why he wasn't around before me makes me want to hurl.

JJ's behavior hasn't stopped there. He also morphed his personality in church to fit a younger audience. He pretended to be the funniest person in church, playing with little kids in front of us. He would get them to laugh and carry on while their parents were trying to focus on the Mass.

He sacrificed the parents' moment to connect with God so he could get their child to laugh. This would rob the parents of the moment of serenity they had with our Lord. Many of these times he risked the child getting into trouble because he got them to misbehave. I would tap him and tell him to stop instigating, yet he continued. He did not care if the parents missed their moment of solitude, and the child risked the chance of getting scolded.

I always felt I had to protect these children and apologize if JJ took it too far. I was embarrassed to be around him some days. I was prepared to run interference when needed, as I wasn't letting a child get spanked or disciplined because the adult behind him wouldn't knock it off.

Reality is crystal clear to me now. He will only care about himself, relieving the same script on repeat. Every person he meets will hear the same lies with different variations to make them meet his needs. No one will ever hear the truth. They will only hear the carefully scripted life he has laid out. If anyone dares question him or dissect what he says, watch out! You'll have hell to pay just like I did. He doesn't like when his carefully groomed prisoners break free.

He has prepared for this moment. He has a slew of manipulation tactics ready to thwart you from breaking free. He's determined the only voice you have will be his. His tactics will make you question your very existence. You will know a solid piece of information, and if it doesn't fit his playbill, he'll gaslight you. He's sneaky, calculated, and spineless. It doesn't matter who you are to him, he'll devastate you. He won't stop until he destroys you. In his fictional reality, you are either his property or enemy numero uno.

So beware when you tango with the snake. His venom is deadly, his eyes are empty, and his soul is vacant. He is only there to squeeze the very breath from your lungs, watch as your body slinks to the ground, and he slithers out the door as his venom stunts your system. He thinks he has won, but the battle has only begun.

29

SACRIFICE

There is beauty in the sacrifice. It may not feel like it now, but everything you did has a purpose. Everything you executed in your daily lives has a meaning, whether you can see it or not. If you're anything like me, you want all the answers, but the thing is ... we don't need all the answers.

Don't get me wrong: having all the answers might help us analyze each situation until we're blue in the face, but it doesn't change the facts. As much as we would like, we can't change our past. There are no do-overs in life. We have one shot, and we have to do our best.

I know this because I blamed myself for everything that went wrong in my marriage. I never let the narrow-minded man I married take responsibility for anything. Well, until I started healing. I would love to change the fact my ex-husband of almost fourteen years had multiple cell phone lines and at one point, I came across a number I didn't recognize. Sure, we had extra lines for the iPads that the kids played on where they would destroy each other's Minecraft houses, but the unknown number wasn't for those.

Lord, help us. The kids would bring their fights into the real world. Please tell me I'm not alone in this. Then we would have to put the iPads in timeout while they reconnected on a human level. Seriously, I can't be the only parent who's had to tell their kids to stop blowing up their siblings' houses or stealing food or any other inanimate object for that matter. Anyways, my ex's bill included a brand-new phone. It wasn't my phone, and it wasn't his, but it did have his phone number registered as the main point of contact on the account. I didn't like that fact; however, it's the truth. I would have been better off not knowing because it didn't help my situation, and it didn't make me feel better. So, you see, we don't need all the answers even if we think we do.

Gut punch

When you get all the answers, you think it will make you feel better. You might think you can fix what happened or you can find a way to take the blame because this is how you've addressed conflict for the totality of your life. You want there to be something you missed. You think if you take the blame like you almost always do, then life can go back to the way it was. Maybe you think it is better to be the martyr and save someone else from taking the blame. Blunt fact: that little martyrdom you have going on is helping no one.

Let's chop this up. When you take the blame, why are you doing it? Are you seeking validation? Are you trying to eliminate the conflict so everyone can be "happy" again? Newsflash, no one is happy when conflict goes unresolved. They just bury it, only to bring it up another day or scowl at someone from across the room. Better yet, if this is a child, they grow into a person who thinks they are never wrong.

They also think no one should ever disagree with them, or they will become aggressive and belligerent when you refuse to meet their demands. When you receive a phone call from them, they scream so much you can't get a word in because they haven't gone to therapy, and screaming at you once every six months feels good because in their minds, you "deserve" it. Then they hang up without giving you a chance to have a real adult conversation.

Trust me, it's messy. I have one of those children, and it's not pretty. So, figure out why you let people treat you like a dumping ground. Look in the mirror and get real with yourself. Get down to the nitty-gritty of why you're doing something.

I know this may seem a little harsh, but I can say it because I've been there. Taking responsibility for someone's hooey isn't living. It's making yourself small and invisible to those around you. You could be the matriarch of your family, but no one is going to follow your lead when you're playing small. You weren't birthed to be small. You were created to take up space and be the freaking badass God sent you here to be.

From here on out, your status is a badass, and it's time for you to strut accordingly. I hope you're feeling me on this. Step into your purpose. You're not a martyr or a saint. It's time to put down your savior mentality and be your badass self.

Boundaries

These have been my saving grace for the last few years. I haven't perfected them, but I'm getting better every day. I don't know what experience you've had or have not had with these, so allow me to introduce you to them.

A boundary is <u>not</u> something you utilize to manipulate someone or to coerce them to do what you want. It's not a means to control someone.

An example of what a boundary is not: "If you don't stop posting about XYZ on your social media pages because I don't like it, you can't talk to me anymore. You won't be allowed to come to my events, be around my family, or even on my school property."

This is not a boundary because the person in this situation is attempting to manipulate the other person. They are trying to coerce them to get them to do what they want. I wouldn't recommend doing this because no one will walk away happy. If possible, it would be better to have a direct conversation, in person, between the individuals who are in disagreement. You also shouldn't involve other people if those people tend to blow things out of proportion. Let's face it, some people like drama and are only there to "win" an argument. When these types of people get involved, there will be no resolution, only more conflict.

An example of what a boundary is: "I understand you don't like what I'm posting on my social media pages. I will not be changing what I write or say in my video content, but if it bothers you, then I'd suggest you not look at it anymore."

This is straight to the point. The person in this scenario is honoring both sides of the conversation. There is no coercion, and this person invites the other not to look at the content. If someone is bothered by the content that is being posted, then they should practice self-control, especially when looking at content that hurts their own feelings. This is not the responsibility of the person posting but the person who keeps choosing to read it and hurt their own feelings. They are especially responsible for hurting their own feelings when you've blocked them from your account, and they get on another account to creep on your page. That's on them, not you.

Which brings me to my next point. Social media can be tricky when you have family members who don't connect with you in the real world but want to stalk your social media and then blow your phone up, harassing you about what you're posting. Before you get upset about their nasty texts and phone calls, remember their behavior has more to do with them than it does you. If you want to heal openly and talk about the trauma you've experienced, go for it. Just be prepared if someone tries to manipulate you.

Stand your ground and own your voice. If you "lose" someone, they weren't meant to be in your life any longer because what is for you won't leave you or pass you by.

Boundaries should be used to help you keep yourself in check, knowing what you will and will not put up with. This is to help you stay true to yourself. However, if someone repeatedly harasses you because of what you did or didn't do, then it is time to restrict their access to you in all forms.

Text messages

Ahh, the beauty of text messages. You can send and receive messages within seconds, but the reality if you open them is up to you. Confession time, I don't always open my texts. If I do, sometimes I open them but don't read them, or sometimes I delete the message altogether if it's from someone or their family member who has been off their rocker and escaped the psych ward. Just kidding, no one has been to the psych ward yet, but it wouldn't hurt if they vacationed there, especially after the insanity at Disney World. Yikes, the insecurities revealed themselves there but I'll spare you the details.

I never know these days what I'll receive. One day we're good and getting along, then the next day I have some unchained person foaming at the mouth, telling me not to talk to my stepchildren. Okay, let's put a pin in this until you simmer down.

My ex-family can be intense and controlling along with their following. It's sad they don't see what's going on, but when they do or act like they want them to, they are just puppets that are played with. Some days I like them and some days I walk right on by. They are the type of people I use boundaries with. I'm guessing you might have a few of those in your life too. So, no matter who you are around, you can use boundaries. Remember, they're your boundaries, and it's up to you how to use them.

Financial independence

Through the last few years, I've learned what it means to make major sacrifices. Before getting divorced, I paid for almost everything on my own, and this prepared me for life after divorce. It was one of the best gifts I could have ever given myself. Before trouble reared its ugly head, I started investing in myself. I attended business conferences and a variety of master classes. This allowed me to reconnect with my inner self. This allowed me to rediscover what I needed in life. I finally got to put the focus back on myself.

Attending these classes allowed me to connect with individuals who developed a high level of personal development who knew there was more to life than the run of the mill 9-5 rat race. I took these opportunities to grow and stretch my mind. It allowed me to reconnect with the little girl who wanted more out of life than being an educator who worked her butt off but was still broke and working a minimum of forty-six hours a month overtime off the clock. I wasn't only broke, but my administrators disrespected me and treated me like garbage. I knew there was more to life than this, so I kept digging. I wanted something better.

My next move was the biggest sacrifice I decided to make. I sold my house and everything in it. I did this so I could pay my bills and the debts JJ stuck me with. Once he moved out, he wouldn't help me with anything, and he didn't come back to pick up the rest of his stuff so I had to make moves others wouldn't. To be completely honest, I think God asked me to do this because He knew these things were holding me back.

Once I sold everything and I got out of my house, I felt free. The last two boxes I took out of my house were old pictures of JJ, Cece, Barb, and Mitch. I would have trashed them, but I had respect for Mitch. I didn't want to throw his memories in the trash, even though he has been gone over ten years now. He was my best friend. I loved him a lot, and I wanted to give his memories back to the family that now treats me like an enemy because I speak the truth about what happened to me.

You see, when I gave up my house and all the things in it, I was getting back in alignment with God. I was out of position and by obeying and doing what He told me, I had a chance at recovering what I had lost twofold. By trusting God with my life and heart, He finally got first place. The sacrifice was worth it. It was hard watching everything I worked so hard for get loaded into other people's cars or be donated, but the freedom I've gained from letting everything go is so incredibly freeing.

I barely recognize my life. I have the freedom to live the way I want. Plus, I only have about $15,000 left in debt to pay off, then I'll be totally free. This doesn't include the $250,000 in debt I paid off all by myself while I was married. I'm not saying this to gloat, but I'm sharing this to give you hope. I want to give you hope no matter what type of situation you're in. Just in case you're wondering, I made under $28,000 a year, and I had to work every summer.

Silver linings

Earlier, I mentioned that through focusing on myself, I reconnected with the little girl I once was. I started learning what she needed and what the woman I have become wants. I've spent my time investing in myself not only financially but in self-care.

Self-care seems like a hot topic these days, and it should be. Each person is a whole entire person all by themselves. We don't need to have kids to be important or be married or to be validated by the president. Okay, the president probably doesn't care if I'm taking care of myself, but in my world, I am the queen of me. I'm a princess of the Most High God, and I'll be taking care of myself. I would encourage you to do the same.

Some things I've done to take care of myself and heal from the trauma I experienced:

1. Connect with God and read scripture.
2. Forgive myself for not understanding what I was going through.
3. Allowed myself lots of time to sleep.
4. I went to the spa—I highly recommend deep tissue massages and facials. These are sooooo nice. A full spa day is pretty sweet too.
5. Exercise—I hired a personal trainer for extra support.
6. I put myself and my needs first.
7. I focused on my growth-read books, learned something new.
8. Explored nature—disconnected from the world and took in the views around me. Allowed myself to get grounded and naturally regulated my body.

9. I made a list of all the things I've ever wanted to do and did them.
10. Took several extended vacations a year—4x a year—This is my favorite self-care "strategy."
11. Bought myself flowers
12. Started singing again
13. Took dancing lessons—spinning around the room with a strong dance partner is so much fun!
14. I went to dinner by myself.
15. Painted
16. Drove on back roads listening to music.
17. Took bubble baths with candles and wine.
18. Went to the beach and spent time with my best friend.

No matter how you heal, just make sure you take the time to do it; otherwise, you might find yourself in the same type of relationship with a different person. You are worth so much more than bread-crumbs and lazy love. It's time to love yourself and give YOU everything you've always wanted and needed.

30

DETOURS

Have you ever had your heart broken or landed in a situation you wish you could have changed?

Did you mull it over after it was finished? You know where the door is shut and sealed never to be opened again ... and there you stand, trying to pry it open with your fingernails, looking for a way to make it better. You think if you could go back and "fix" just one more thing, it could have changed the trajectory of your life.

I've been there. I've been there so MANY times, it's nauseating. My mother says I'm tenacious, and others say I'm plain, old stubborn. As for me, I think I have iron-clad willpower. I decide I'm going to do something, and I go for it. I don't wait around, I just go.

It's kinda like when I decided to go skydiving for my thirtieth birthday. I had two planes reserved for a group of twelve to jump out of a perfectly good plane, but most backed out because they were too scared. I say to hell with being scared.

Being scared comes from fear. Fear comes from the pit of hell to keep us from being the people we were meant to be. I got my jump gear on and went. I'm serious, if you get on YouTube and search for "Kelly Franklin Tandem Skydive," you'll find me. Plus, I'm going to let you in on a little secret, I'm scared of heights and flying. I still jumped out of a perfectly good plane right above a storm cloud at 12,000 feet. There might have been a little push from my jump instructor, but I still did it.

Jumping out of a plane is the most badass thing I've ever done. At first, my stomach dropped, and I felt like I was going to suffocate. I couldn't breathe with how hard the wind was smacking me in the face, but once my instructor pulled the ripcord and the parachute popped out, catapulting me upwards, then all of a sudden, my perspective changed. I wasn't scared anymore. I could breathe, and I was enjoying my new view.

I would turn from the left to the right, steering the parachute in the direction my instructor needed it to go. He had a fancy watch that guided our every move. The safety this provided made me feel much better. I got to see farmers' fields from up high, and ultimately, I pulled my legs up, landing in the field on my butt while the ground crew was there to catch us as the wind kept pushing us along. The wind was so strong had they not been there, I could have been telling you a different story. It's okay to allow other people to help you.

Not everything I experienced during my skydiving adventure was something I planned. It didn't go at all how I planned it; however, it did go the way it was supposed to.

The fact of the matter is life doesn't always go how you planned. From my experience, it does go how it's supposed to.

I know, I know ... there's probably someone like my former self groaning because you want to control life and you think you're in control; well, you're not. At some point, you're going to have to get used to this fact or you don't have to, but it still won't change the fact you will never be in control.

I fondly call this a detour. Think about the detour signs we see on the road. It's not something we want to see, but it will help so we don't run our car into a chuck hole as we speed down the road. At that moment, we need the road crew there to guide us on another path. This detour will help us. That's the same thing that happens when God points us in another direction. He points us in the direction we need to go. This may not be the direction we wanted to go, but He can see farther ahead, and this is the way He knows we need to proceed.

So, we can't always be in control. I'm thankful I finally learned how to stop controlling every part of my life. This has allowed me to give God true control in my life, and the detours He has taken me on have helped me heal broken parts within me, and He also has directed me to the people I need in my life.

It's true. I never thought I'd love anyone again, ever. I never thought I would feel any inkling of love at all from anyone in any capacity, but I have. I met a man named Liam, and he turned my world upside down and inside out, in a good way.

Meet Liam

The moment I started talking to Liam, it has been an adventure. In a world where dating has been full of F this or that guys and girls, I wanted something real. I wanted to be with someone real. I wanted to date a man who is real and honest with himself as I am with myself. And he's definitely the man I've been praying for, even if just for this moment.

Our first date and the second were filled with fireworks. The way I felt when I first met him was nothing I had ever felt before. I don't mean I had butterflies in my stomach; it was actually the opposite. I felt comfortable with him. I felt for the first time if ever I could be my true self.

In past relationships, I did myself a disservice by hiding parts of myself. I didn't with him. I let my crap all hang out, and he didn't go running.

We spent our first date at one of my favorite places, and he didn't stare at his phone the whole night. He didn't huff or puff at me when I made a request, and I even let him drive my car. I never let anyone drive my car. Oh my goodness, and he opened my door and treated me like a lady. I don't know about you, but I love when a man is a real man, and he knows how to treat a lady.

I enjoyed riding shotgun and holding his hand as we drove down the street, talking and relishing in each other's company. It was so refreshing. Plus, the way he held me when he kissed me for the first time was thrilling. I never thought I could feel the way I felt at that moment, ever. I thought my sex drive had died but clearly, it had not! Wozers!

Our second date was even better. I was fortunate enough to meet his close friends and spend the night hanging out on a double date. I'm sure they were vetting me, but I don't care. I had a blast! We went to a charming restaurant that had scrumptious pasta, and Liam dripped salsa on his menu. When I wiped his menu off with a napkin, he said, "Thank you, Momma." He didn't know this, but he struck a vulnerable heart cord when he said this. It was what JJ used to call me. Don't get me wrong; I liked it, but it just hit me in a super vulnerable place.

He also told me he and his friends share food when they go out to eat so we were literally eating off each other's plates. When it came to his plate though, he fed me off his fork. Ummm, yes please. I've been treated so poorly, I felt like a queen when I was out with him. I felt like the only woman in the room. I've heard about women being treated like this but to be one of them was amazing.

After dinner, we drove around, trying to find somewhere to go bowling. In Indiana, it was still cold at this point in the year, and a spot to bowl was hard to come by. I didn't care how far we drove as long as I was sitting next to him. Every time his buddy drove to a new place, he checked in to make sure it was good with me. It was nice to be considered when someone else was making a decision. I had been invisible for so long, it was nice to be seen.

When we finally found a place to bowl, the men had the ladies sit down first. WHAT?! Seriously, I got to sit down and put my snazzy bowling shoes on first while the guys stood up. I've been wanting to have a weekend where I felt like a million bucks, and this was it.

I paid for nothing. I didn't know there were still men in this universe who would pay for a lady and not gripe about it. I honestly didn't know how to respond. I tried to take care of things, in my masculine energy on the first date, and was respectfully shot down. Then on this date, I got to remain in my feminine energy the whole time. Being in this energy was amazing to me.

I got to be on a date with a man who gave me all his attention, and when I went to sit in my own chair, he had me come sit on his lap and lean on him. He held me and was happy I was taking up space in his life. Talk about shaking a woman's life up. This was it.

I've felt like garbage for so long. I felt so unworthy when it came to a man, this right here healed a part of me that I didn't even know needed healing. I knew my worth at this moment before he came along but to let someone in who sees my worth too was mind boggling to me.

I've had to fight for a seat in the front for so long that to be given one was refreshing to me. To spend my time with a man who is genuine and real with me was life changing. I want you to understand Liam. I want you to get a glimpse of who he is. When my shoe came untied, he tried to stop me from bowling. Haha! I didn't know this was bad luck, but when I got back to my seat, I leaned down to tie my shoe. He stopped me. He didn't let me tie my own shoe. He tied it for me. Something so simple meant so much to me. He didn't know it then, but he was changing my view of how I should be treated. He changed my view on how I should have been treated.

This weekend was thrilling for me. I'm not going to share everything that happened, but he opened up a part of me I thought was gone forever. I never thought I could love anyone again, and the fact I started to like him a little was exciting for me. It was exciting because of how good and true his heart really is. It was exciting because I could feel a part of me I thought had passed away never to return again. I will always cherish my time with him.

I don't know where this adventure will go but I'm glad I had the courage to take the chance. I'm glad I put myself out there. I'm thankful he held my hand and heart. I'm thankful he showed me the good that can still be found in this world. I'm glad I know I can still possess the ability to love someone and because of him, my heart is a little bigger. I like his friends too. They showed me kindness I've not experienced in a very long time. They will always have a special place in my heart.

So, embrace the detours in your life. You may not know where they are taking you but just know it will take you to where you are supposed to be.

31

TRANSFORMATION

"Remember not the events of the past, the things of the long ago consider not; See I am doing something new! Now it springs forth, do you not perceive it? In the wilderness I make a way, in the wasteland, rivers. Wild beasts honor me, jackals and ostriches, For I put water in the wilderness and rivers in the wasteland for my chosen people to drink, The people whom I formed for myself, that they might recount my praise." (Isaiah 43:18-21, The Catholic Study Bible. Third Edition)

As I sat in church yesterday, I listened to my priest speak about the beautiful transformations that can happen in our lives if we allow God to work. If we allow Him the ability to have control creating and designing the specific path for us without us trying to steal the pen. Without us trying to rewrite the story He needs us to carry out in this world to make it a little better.

If you walk away knowing anything about me, the first line of this scripture written above is tattooed on JJ's right forearm. Isaiah 43:18 was a verse he used to control me, and it's a verse God, Himself, used to recreate me.

You see, I was a wild thing when I was in my twenties. It's a harsh judgment of myself but this is how I felt. I broke The Ten Commandments, and I ran my life the way I wanted. I tried to live them, but I couldn't. I didn't respect them, and I thought God had Moses write them to keep me trapped in a world I didn't want to be in. I thought I didn't belong in church, and I thought He wrote the Commandments because He was a mean and nasty God. He was controlling like everyone else in my life or so I thought.

Boy, was I wrong. I was so massively wrong. I misjudged God in every perspective my younger self had. I wanted to be loved, and I thought JJ was the "one" after my ex-fiancé left. He wasn't the one, far from it.

When JJ had this scripture tattooed on his arm, he would try to use it to control me. If I was upset about a situation that happened a few minutes prior, he would look at his arm and say, "It doesn't matter anymore; it's in the past." He wouldn't listen to me. When I would call him out about something that just happened, he would blow me off. Then he quoted this scripture. I would rebuttal to the excuse JJ concocted because God didn't intend for scripture to be used this way.

God didn't intend and would never want scripture being used to keep someone in bondage. When JJ realized his control tactics were no longer working on me, he would RAGE at me. His face turned scarlet red, and his veins popped out of his forehead, shoulders, neck, and his chest. He would scream at me at the top of his lungs, saying, "I know what I said," while clenching his fists tightly. Then he furiously called the dogs to go into another room, slamming the door and shaking the walls. He didn't come out until the next morning.

When I stood my ground, I knew I was making the right decision. He was furious with me for calling him on the carpet about helping Mara with college. He refused, in every way, to help her. He was disgusted at the fact I offered to pay half of the $500 she asked him to help out with. He refused, saying she didn't give him enough time to come up with the money. She was still waiting for it a year later, and he asked me to get her PayPal information so he could send it but never did.

I thought about sending it, but Mara said it wasn't my responsibility. I was going to send it, but I respected her decision. It's hard when your kids grow up. You want to protect them and, at the same time, let them grow up.

Flashing back to her graduation party, I noticed when we were on the way to celebrate, JJ had not gotten her a card. I asked him if he was planning on getting her a card. He grumbled at me and stated, "I'm going to stop and get her one on the way." I'm not so sure he was going to get her a card had I not mentioned it. I still don't know if he signed my name on the card because he wouldn't let me see it. That was up to him but in the end, he will reap what he sows.

The wilderness

As I walked through this valley filled with fire and brimstone, it was then that Jesus hoisted me into His arms and carried me. I felt as though I was losing everything. I worked hard to earn a family that didn't want me. They needed me. They were my assignment, but they didn't want me. They never did. JJ, Mara, Xavier, Piper, and Zoe didn't want the better life that I worked hard to provide. I let it all go. It slipped through my fingers like dry sand on the beach. Everything I worked diligently for was for Jesus, in human form, to carry me into the wilderness so He could change my life.

The way Jesus started changing my life was in little pieces. The turning point was when Mara started her senior year of high school. I was elated for her and everything she would accomplish in her life. I always felt there was greatness within her. A natural-born leader. I wanted her to do everything she put her mind to.

I question her leadership now. After some interactions we have had and the calloused statements she's made, I wonder if she's a natural-born leader or if it was that she was groomed to parent so her parents didn't have to. I know she was robbed of a better childhood than what she had. I tried my best to make up for what her parents refused to or couldn't give her, but it still wasn't enough. In her eyes, it'll never be enough. She yearned for her parents to care, but they were incapable of caring. It is quite the experience being in the same room with both at the same time. Wow, just wow! And that's not a compliment. If you want a show, grab some popcorn and watch. You'll get one.

I was carried into the wilderness. Minuscule things started happening in my life that I prayed for God to bring them to light. I asked him what was happening behind the scenes. I asked Him to show me what was coming, and He did.

The light

As God was showing me through the spiritual actions of Jesus, I began to change. I began to look for Jesus everywhere I went. I mostly found Him in nature. The more I leaned on Him for comfort, the more He revealed Himself to me. I was pulling into my driveway one day, and I was contemplating if God was real. I looked into the sky and saw a cloud shaped in the form of a heart with a capital G carefully printed in the middle. My heart overflowed with joy. I took my dogs inside and quickly snapped a picture upon returning outside.

The cloud quickly dissipated, but I knew God was real. I knew all the little things that were happening were coming from Him. It didn't matter what bad came along because He was teaching me to trust Him. My relationship was changing with Him. He was the man I needed in my life. I couldn't physically see Him, but spiritually He was filling a need that had gone unfulfilled for years.

Relationships

I mentioned my relationship with God had changed. I started to lean into the Holy Trinity and learn the different roles of each person. This is something I had never wanted to learn before because, in my twenty-something-turned-thirty-something mind, it was too scary. So, before I completely turned to them, I turned to the Holy Mother, Mary.

I did. I felt like I was a little elementary kid running to tattle to someone's mother. I wanted and needed to know how to be a great wife and mother. I wanted to know how to be so much better than I already was, so I ran to Jesus's mother. I ran to the only woman who could have my back and improve the woman I already was. I ran to the Mother Society ridiculed. I ran as fast as I could and spiritually threw myself at her feet. I wanted to know the Mother I had always envisioned living among the clouds, never to be reached because somewhere in my young heart, I felt so completely unworthy until I came to her myself.

When I started to read and study the book, *33 Days to Morning Glory*, everything changed. A deacon at a church mission encouraged everyone there to read this, so I did. I slowly began to learn who Mary was and the power within her name. Once I learned who she truly was, I could feel my heart change. I could tap into love I never knew was available before. I felt myself becoming happier, even though my situation wasn't changing. I leaned into her so she could intervene for me when I prayed. God was changing me through the situation at hand. I wasn't getting what I prayed for, but I was getting something better. I was getting a better me than I had never been before.

At times, I called out to her for help. I needed her divine intercession to take place. I could feel a spiritual war going on within my home. I was still learning, and I could feel it. The energy was off in my home, and it shifted whenever JJ returned. Something was wrong.

I often triple-checked my locks at night to keep the enemy out. I wanted to prevent him from stealing, killing, and destroying anything within the walls of my house. The house God had entrusted to me to take care of, but the thief was already inside.

I realized I had been sleeping next to him for years. He came to destroy everything within me because he hated himself to the core. He hated his children and, worst of all, he hated God and thought he was god. He acted as though the kingdom was his, and he had nothing to apologize for. Everything he was and did in his eyes was right. This is the war I was fighting against. This is the war I gave to my Mother Mary and the Holy Trinity. I asked them to drive every evil thing out of my house. They were the ones who protected me at night. They were the only reasons I could sleep. Every night I prayed,

"I lie down in peace altogether, and sleep; For you alone, O Yahweh, Make me dwell in safety" (Psalms 4:8, The Scriptures Bible).

This scripture made me feel safe, and as I invited Mary into my home to protect me, I could sleep soundly. It was during these times JJ couldn't sleep. He told me he woke up in the middle of the night. He had nightmares about his deceased father Mitch appearing to him. The more I prayed and my heart changed, the more he complained he was having these dreams. I offered to listen and talk with him, but he always said he couldn't tell me.

My relationship with God only grew from there. When I felt deeply close to Mary, then I started talking to God and Jesus more. I asked them to show me what I was missing in my life. At one point, they took the screens off my eyes. I always see good in people, but this was the moment Jesus let the screens drop. I saw exactly who JJ was. I recognized he was the evil within my home.

Furthermore, JJ wasn't alone. I felt "things" inside of my house when he wasn't there. I felt deep pressure and anxiety when I would walk in certain places. It felt as though I wasn't supposed to be there. Being in my own home felt strange. I did what any good Catholic would do: I blasted KLOVE in my house. If there's anything evil spirits don't like, it's worship music. Then I would sing at the top of my lungs, praising my BIG GOD and drop to my knees in worship.

It was during these times God showed up big for me. It was in these moments I truly learned I was His daughter, and He chose me. My God is my Father, Provider, and Protector. In these moments, He proved how He would protect me.

I felt like a little girl running to the daddy she needed, and He protected me just like I needed Him to. The bad guys or, in this case, the bad spirits couldn't get to me with God and St. Michael protecting me. They both promised to protect and defend me in spiritual battles, and that's exactly what they did.

Submission

During this season, I learned to submit to God. I knew what submission is and why it was important. I also learned that God is the head, which means the husband is the head. I learned to submit to a husband who was nasty to me. One who refused to speak to me and gave me silent treatment for days on end until he thought I would break.

These types of tactics are abuse. He carefully chose his moves to make certain each manipulation would coerce me to do what he wanted. He wanted me to feel like there was no other way but his. He especially did this in late December 2016, after he had suffered a seizure earlier that summer. It was during this month I wanted a divorce. I couldn't take it anymore. I had turned to some of his family members for help, but they blew me off. They told me I won't be getting a divorce. They told me my actions were going to hurt JJ, but they didn't care how I felt. I felt trapped. They were such enablers and didn't care about me at all.

So, for my Christmas presents, JJ took our twin daughters to the jewelry store to get something for me. It was the only time I got something nice in the nearly fifteen years we were together. "The girls" apparently picked out an upgraded Claddaugh wedding ring and a locket that read "I love you." They apparently wanted to get me one that read "Mom," but they didn't want their bio mom, Karen, to get irate about it. They informed me she easily flew off the handle, and they didn't want to deal with her. I stayed after receiving their gifts. I thought maybe he would get better. Maybe he would become the man I thought God wanted him to be.

Looking back, I would have rather gotten the divorce but when two twelve-year-olds are looking you in the eyes so proud of the gifts they picked, it's hard to walk away. Piper and Zoe smiled so big when they gave me their gifts. They told me to hurry up on putting them on, as they wanted to see me wearing them. God, I loved those kids. This moment will be forever etched in my memory because more than loving my role as wife, I loved being their momma. Unfortunately, they were just pawns to him. They were only there to keep me around a bit longer. Those kids deserved a better dad, and I deserved a better husband. I deserved a husband who actually loved me, not some clown playing games.

Earlier this year, when JJ suffered a seizure and landed in the hospital for three days, his body was, and probably still is, very dependent on alcohol. He had not given his body what it needed to function, so it responded by attacking him.

At this point in time, I was trying to support him by praying for him to come to God with his problems. I was trying my best to be a good wife. The submission calls you to follow the "head" of the house. You follow your husband in the moves he is making. You follow him even if he's making bad moves because God will eventually deal with those choices. This is especially when he's blowing thousands of dollars per month that were supposed to be in our retirement fund or cheating every other weekend to go on a "guys trip" to get counseling because he can't handle life, and he wants to have good friends and being a better man.

Even in those times when you honor your husband, allowing himself to hang himself out to dry, God sees your attempts to honor him. This is when God gives you glory as a wife. This is when God honored me and drove that wicked man out of my home so He could deal with him.

Prayers for future women

It was during this time God proved to me I was different from JJ's former partners. Many people become bitter when they've been hurt and cheated on. I can look at one of his exes, and it's written all over her face. She can't stand that he cheated on her. This has trapped her, and, in a way, he will always have power over her until she forgives and releases him. The other one made off-the-wall comments about if we didn't work out. Maybe she was actually preparing me in a backward way, which actually helped in the end, but I pray for all the future women that might get involved with him.

I pray they get away from him. I don't want anyone to be hurt the way I have been. I don't want someone to think they have found "The One." I don't want another woman to think, *Thank you God for bringing this wonderful man into my life.* Let's be honest, and this was my thought, but he was only reflecting my personality and he studied me hard because he has copied my personality. Sometimes it's scary how much he has copied my personality.

So, the "man" you think you're getting is actually me. I'm the "man" and woman of the house. I guess I actually made him a little better. Glad I could help you out. Do be careful when he starts helping out with no strings attached because there are strings, and abuse will be attached to those strings.

But as for the other women I've talked to … yes, they did background checks on him and searched me up. One even admitted she flew into Indiana and rode in the Jeep down our street so she could see where I lived. She found me, and it made for an awkward conversation. I should say awkward conversations because multiple women looked me up. They wanted answers as to who JJ really is. I had to break several hearts, but at least I could help them get away. I'm glad I could help them find freedom when they felt trapped.

This is how I know I'm different than his bitter lovers from the past. I want to help other women while they just watched my life go down the tubes, and our kids were a part of the hurt. Sick people watch their kids get hurt. That's one thing I'll never be able to wrap my head around.

The other women

Talking to these other women wasn't surprising. I knew in my heart something was going on since I was thirty, and now I'm way past that. JJ covered it up so well I couldn't find his lies. I knew what my body was telling me, but he was always there with a "word" salad to contradict my feelings or what my gut was telling me. A "word" salad is when he talked in circles about random things to confuse me. Being in a relationship with him was much like living with a five-year-old who always wanted his way. If he didn't get his way, then you were the one who was at fault.

This rang true when these women contacted me. I won't share the screenshots because that could put their lives in jeopardy, but when he showed up at the apartment with "their" things in a box, crying hysterically and saying, "This is the worst thing I've ever done," it was insane. Everything he has done is insane. He even showed up at one woman's work demanding his apartment key back, but yet he still had her expensive work equipment. She told me that her manager had to walk him off the property and make sure he left. This tells me she was his next "supply," and she was going to be his next victim.

Yet, with my help, she interrupted his process of grooming her into victimhood. He threw a fit over a key, but he had her work belongings. That's probably because I got our computer in the divorce, so he took hers because he had to save some face in the divorce and try to be the "good guy" again.

You see, there's no winning when you screw multiple women over, especially when one of them is me. I'm going to help every woman I can to get away from abusive, manipulative, controlling men who thinks the world owes him because he has "mommy" issues. I'm going to keep standing up for myself and women in general. You don't get to screw people over and act like the victim. We are the real victims, and that is why they came to me. They wanted a woman who has the guts to speak up. This is why I confronted you about cheating on me with the affair partner in Wisconsin on the phone when you walked in the door with your head down. I confronted you earlier that year in July, and you responded with "I don't even have enough for one woman, let alone two." I couldn't agree more.

JJ, you're a coward, and your mommy issues are your problem, not ours. You are sick and twisted, and you need help. Thank you for setting me free. Thank you for breaking my heart and teaching me what a man does not do. It's time you stopped preying on single women, single moms with young children, or anyone you think will give you a "supply." You need help.

As for the other women, I'm glad I got to meet you. Those of you I met seem like pretty stand-up women, and I hope you have a good life. Let's hope your future relationships go way better than it did with JJ. I wouldn't wish that on any of you.

As for God and I, we are pretty tight, and any future man I date will have to go through Him first. Remember, life isn't defined by what has happened to you, but it's what you make of it. We all met in a pretty screwed-up way, so let's never meet this way again. I wish you ladies all the best.

32

MY SINGLE SEASON

At first my single season seemed daunting. I was asked if I was going to date or get married again, and the thought of either of those two made me want to vomit. I understand when you break up or, worse, get a divorce, in my case, those who care about you want to check in. They want to see where your head is, and these types of questions help them know where you're at in the process.

Thankfully, I'm taking this single season slowly. I've always been the woman who hits the gas pedal in relationships but not this time. I have nothing to prove to anyone. I believe once someone knows their worth, they have more options. They don't have to keep the first guy who asks them out on a date after a divorce. There's way more to life than dating. Plus, dating this day in age is for the birds. It sucks, and I'm not going to have a roster full of men to take my pick from. Gross. I know who I want, and I'm not going to stop until I meet him.

Notice I didn't say find. You can find any guy that doesn't know what he wants but a man who knows his worth and wants a woman to match that ... Oh, yea. This is how you turn a woman on. A confident man who knows what he truly wants, so freaking sexy.

Thank God, I'm Single

There I said it. THANK GOD!

I'm currently single and can live my life according to my hopes, dreams, and goals. I get it if you're not thankful for where you might be residing in life. I can understand if this is not where you want to be. I'd just like you to know it can get better.

I say this because my life has gotten way better since JJ ran out on me. I've been able to live my life the way I've only dreamed of. In the last ten months, I've been on four vacations. This many vacations in such a short time was not possible when I was married. I don't have anyone else to concern myself with except for me. The kids are taken care of, I no longer have pets that are my responsibility, and my cheating ex is his own problem now.

Being single has been a blessing in disguise. I can go where I want and spend time with who I choose. When someone needs me, I can decide if I want to be their go-to person or not. I get to be the person who shows up because I have nothing holding me back. I can live a life of freedom because God Himself decided I deserved a better life. He knew what I wrote on the inside of my heart, and He made it happen.

While being single may have been hard at first, I really like what it has provided me. I'm happy I get to live the life I've always dreamed of. Best of all, I get to make new memories in the way I want to. I get to do life my way. Freedom is amazing!

Single is an opportunity, not a death sentence.

Take time to really get to know yourself. Learn what you want out of this life. Take time to write out your ideal man or woman. Get serious about it. Now that you know what that man looks like, write down every deal-breaker you can think of. What are your biggest turn-ons? What are your biggest turn-offs?

Oh, and one of my biggest red flags is the guy who is always posting muscle selfies on social media. Beware of them. I get it, all of these guys might not be bad, but if you have to constantly post muscle selfies for validation and confidence boosts, what are you doing with your life? Eww! Just walk away or better yet, RUN! These picture ooze insecurities, and you are one hell of a woman who deserves a man who is confident. You don't want a man child who tags models and says, "You are not alone in your workout today." Let alone tagging a married woman in the post. Gross ... are you picking up on whom you shouldn't be dating? I hope so.

Single is a blessing, and it's time you take advantage of it.

Research yourself. Dig deep, and if you put in the time to get to know you, you will start attracting the people who will lead you to the right man.

I'm not saying your journey will be easy, but it will be worth it.

Go change your world, girl!

You are worth it!

THE BEAUTIFUL

33

A LETTER TO JJ

Dear JJ,

The time I spent with you was worth it. I wasn't looking for love, and I thought I had found it in you. Sadly, this turned out to be false. You abused me terribly, and I didn't deserve it. No one deserves to be put through hell as you put me through. What I did realize is the beautiful children you never wanted are the loves I've always dreamed of. You married me, promising to give me biological or adoptive children, a promise you never followed through on. Motherhood seemed fleeting, and it found me through them.

The miracles you took for granted were my blessings. You know that, or at least I hope you do. The children God gave me are better than I could have ever imagined. I'm so glad God brought them into my life.

The rotten part is you're missing out on knowing some extraordinary people. People God specifically chose you for, and you discarded them and me like trash. If you wake up one day and feel alone, remember you chose this. You threw your family away. My blinders are off, and even though we had good times, I know it was a façade. I was the good in our marriage. I was spontaneous and fun you were a copycat who didn't have a solid foundation. This makes me feel sad for you, but it's not an excuse to hurt the kids or me.

You never deserved us. Enjoy your scripted world, as you'll soon forget us if you haven't already. We know you live your life with deleted scenes. Enjoy the quiet, plot twists, money, lies, infidelity, cheating, stealing, emptiness, and new supply you're chasing every few seconds. Just keep in mind, this world will eventually run out. You'll have to answer for the wrongs you've chosen. You'll be forced to remember you had a family that loved you unconditionally when the film strip races past your eyes, but you chose worldly desires over loving us and God.

I understand you never wanted us, but you needed us.

From the ex-wife you loved to hate and abused for pleasure,

I hope one day you'll make peace with your past and be the person God sent you here to be. Being vulnerable and authentic is where those rare moments exist. The ones that change our lives forever.

Be rare, JJ. I still believe there is good inside of you; it's just buried under a lot of hurt. It's okay to make a mistake, and it's okay to ask for forgiveness. There's nothing wrong in that.

It's okay to be real, and it's okay to be you. It's even okay to believe in the scripture you had tattooed on your arm. You seek validation and permission so here it is: take that scripture seriously. Pursue it.

God is waiting for you to let Him in.

It's all up to you.

Love,

Kelly

Ps. I forgive you and release you. #BeautifullyBrokenKF

34

A LETTER TO MY CHILDREN

To my children: Mara, Xavier, Piper, and Zoe

Always remember your earthly parents will never be perfect. When we fail you or you feel like we have failed you, look up to your heavenly Father. He is perfect in every way, and He loves you more than any of us ever could. Please take the time to heal so the pain won't impact future generations. Be so audacious in your healing that it impacts future generations for the better.

I did my best, and God has the rest.

I'll love you forever and more than you could ever imagine. No matter what happens between us, I hope life is good for you.

Love always,

Kelly aka Momma

#BeautifullyBrokenKF

35

A LETTER TO A FUTURE OVERCOMER

Dear Future Overcomer,

      I'm glad this letter found you. If you're currently fighting to get sober, please know I believe in you. Anything is possible when you give your life to God, and there is nothing so awful that you've done in your life that it can't be fixed. You're not so powerful you are able to mess up the plan God has for you.

If you read my book, then you know I'm the ex-wife of an addict. He taught me a lot about being an addict without physically instructing me. By watching JJ's torment over the last almost fifteen years, I can understand why someone would become dependent on drugs, nicotine, or alcohol. Through JJ's struggles, compassion grew in my heart for people like him.

I don't condemn you; I'd like to help you. I know there's an ability deep within you to heal what has been broken inside of you. I believe in you. Be strong and courageous. You can do ALL things through Christ who strengthens you. He has a plan to prosper you and not to harm you. All you have to do is invite him into your life. Open the door of your heart and invite Him in.

He's waiting on you, and I want to learn about your success. I hope that you will have the courage to invest in your future the same way God chose you. The way He knitted you together in your mother's womb because you were chosen and selected to be in this world.

No matter what you've done, God still needs you. He still wants you.

You are loved, chosen, and worthy of this life that has been gifted to you.

Your healing is waiting for you.

All my love,

Kelly Franklin

#BeautifullyBrokenKF

36

A LETTER TO JJS AFFAIR PARTNERS

To my ex-husband's affair partners,
Yes, you were not the only one. I know this.

I see you. I see a person who may or may not have known about my marriage with my ex-husband. You may have thought you were genuinely dating someone who was divorced and single, but the hard truth is he wasn't. He very much lived a double life and probably more. You were never his, and he was never yours. You weren't married to him. You didn't have children with him, and if you did, you need to let us know you did. We still want our family intact, no matter how "Jerry Springer" it is. You know this situation is twisted and together, we can make it better.

What I want you to know is I'm not mad at you if you truly thought you were dating someone who was single and available. This isn't on you. My ex knew what he was doing. It was planned, calculated, and executed to serve him and only him. He set out to destroy you like he tried to destroy me. You got away, good for you.

If you were, however, dating him and knew full well he was married, you need help. Trying to steal someone's husband is evil. When you came into my house and saw our wedding pictures on the wall, what were you thinking? When you saw pictures of my children and had sex with my husband, what were you thinking? That's on you. Carry this lesson with you and learn from it. You partook in evil, and you should have never stepped into my house. You know you fulfilled Satan's plan by doing this. I'm disgusted at your actions and his actions. I have forgiven you and released both of you. Do better. Be better. And stop hurting people's families.

What you sow will come back to you. You can't have sex with someone's husband and expect them to not cheat on you. You can't expect them to be faithful to you. You can't have sex with him and expect the kids to want to be a part of your life. Trashy people cheat with someone's husband. Are you trash? This is your wake-up call to change your life. Even if you're addicted to alcohol or drugs, you can change now and do better. You have to choose, and you can if you want to. Heal what is broken within you. A better life is waiting for you if you want it.

I don't hate you. I hurt for you. I hurt that you think so little of yourself that this is who you've become. You don't have to be this person. I forgive and release you.

If you're one of the ones who thought he was truly single and available, I forgive and release you as well. We don't have to be friends, but know I've prayed for you. I know it wasn't easy when you found out about me, my children, and our fur babies. I know it must have sucked when you found out you had a part in destroying a family. It must have hurt so much when your heart shattered into a billion pieces. But sweetheart, know this, you're better than this. This situation is not your fault, and it's not your sin. You don't need to carry this with you. If anything, I have a love for you. I know the man who I loved and was married to. I'm glad you got away. Good for you. I'm glad you didn't suffer the way I did or at least I hope you didn't.

Now please take the time to heal yourself and put your pieces back together. You are worthy and were made for love. Please know I believe there is someone out there for you, someone who will love you from the depths of their soul to the top of their heart. I bet we'd get along if we had the chance to meet. I'm sure you might have a huge heart and you love hard. I'm guessing this because that's how I am. I wish you well in this world. You deserve better. You should be loved, so go love yourself first. Truly learn how you need to be loved and spend time with yourself. I only want what's good for you in this world.

Kindest regards,
Kelly Franklin
#BeautifullyBrokenKF

APPENDIX

37

RESOURCES FOR HELP

National Domestic Violence Hotline
800-799-7233
SMS: Text START to 88788

Suicide and Crisis Lifeline

38

ACKNOWLEDGMENTS

First and foremost, I want to thank God. My Father in Heaven who has been with me throughout my life. He has always been by my side and held the pen crafting the most unique adventure for me on this Earth. Thank you for teaching me how to love and what it means to love. Through your example, I've learned to become the woman I'm supposed to be. Thank you for walking me through the darkest moments in my life carrying me when I was too fragile to walk. You're my rock whom I will always trust. I wish I would have put my Faith in you much sooner. Thank you times a million for never giving up on me.

Eli Gonzalez- Thank you for teaching me how to write and for holding my hand throughout this process. You are an amazing teacher and I appreciate everything you've taught me. Without your guidance, I'm not sure this book would exist. I'm so thankful for everything you've done and for allowing me the opportunity to partner with you and publish my book.

The Ghostwriting Team- Thank you for helping me create a book that reflected my vision. From the front cover to the back cover and everything in between. Your talent is unmatched and I'm thankful for everything you've done.

Sharon T.- I could write a book on you alone. Thank you for choosing to give me life. A life God had specifically entrusted to you, as my mother. Motherhood is no small feat and you've done a wonderful job! I appreciate you driving me to school and teaching me to pray. I didn't understand what you were teaching me then but I do now. I know God is bigger than every circumstance that arises in life. Thank you for helping guide my relationship with Him and supporting me through the hardest season in my life. I know it wasn't easy but we did it.

Ann T.- Thank you for keeping me afloat while I was drowning. Thank you for taking my calls in the middle of the night and sleeping over just so you knew I was safe. I appreciate you bringing groceries and baking pizza when I was refusing to eat because life as I knew it had ended. I'm thankful you're my sister and I'm glad God put you in my life. You're the best!

Michael T.- Thank you for teaching me about cars and giving me those big brother pep talks. It was needed and appreciated. Thank you for showing up on the worst of days with Long's Donuts. You know how to cheer me up.

My niece & nephew- Thank you for teaching me to be a better person. Both of you are extraordinary people who have so much to offer this world. You both have been specifically selected and chosen by God, himself, to grace this world with your presence. This world would be empty without you or the joy you bring me. Thank you for making me laugh and giving me a purpose. I know both of you will do amazing things with your life.

Tami F.- Thank you for being the best friend I could have ever asked for. You are a gift from God. You've been there for me through thick and thin. You've shown me what it means to be a true friend. I appreciate it when you attend Mass with me and tell me you want "Cheez-its," but I told you it was Jesus. You make life fun! I'm thankful God placed you in my life and I'm glad we're on this adventure together. Thank you for being my family. I love you!

Austin F.- Thank you for making me laugh, being my friend and a big brother to me. Thank you for including me in your family and teaching me how to swim in the ocean. Thank you for being there for me through the highs and lows as well as giving me a safe place to land. You and Tami are angels on Earth. I'm so incredibly thankful for both of you.

Braydon St. Clair- Thank you for guiding me into a world that felt scary and unknown. The gym used to be intimidating and with your instruction, I no longer feel afraid when I step into this space. I feel confident and ready to go. You're talent and efforts are appreciated. Thank you for helping me get back to the me I love.

Erika Dale-Thank you for supporting me and being a shoulder to lean on during my darkest time. Your counsel, encouragement, and prayers helped more than you know. I'm so glad I have you in my life. Your example and presence in my life mean more than you know.

Kristin Richards-Thank you for ministering to me while I learned to navigate the murky waters of divorce. When my life imploded it was your words and support that carried me to places I wouldn't have dared to go. Your counsel brought clarity and direction. Thank you for always being one phone call away.

Jesse Dale & Erik Richards- Thank you for showing me there are still good men in this world who genuinely care about others. Your kind words, example, and faith inspire me.

Tammy Price- Thank you for being my first business coach and friend. You were the one I opened up to when I was learning how to change old habits. It's true what they say about old habits dying hard because you challenged my broke mindsets to the point of frustration. That frustration set me up for a comeback I didn't know was coming. The things in life that appeared to be giant mountains turned out to be ant hills with your help. Overall, my life is profoundly different because of your efforts. I appreciate you and thank you for everything you've done for me. I'm so grateful God placed you in my life.

Xtina Harmsworth- It was your audacious coaching that snapped me out of the cognitive dissonance I had been stuck in for years. The abuse I went through caused me to shut down completely staying in a "freeze" reaction but when I heard you for the first time, you helped me reconnect with my younger self. You helped me realize I could believe in myself and pursue my dreams as well. You helped me realize the life I was living was not what I wanted. I wanted more. Thank you for your guidance, coaching, energy, and spirit. You brought me back to reality and I will be forever grateful for your presence in my life.

Kati Elliot- Thank you for coaching me and asking the deep questions I didn't know I needed to ask myself. This helped me prepare for my future and I greatly appreciate you. Thank you for being in my corner.

Aunt Linda- Thank you for sending me handwritten cards filled with scripture and letting me know you're thinking of me. The words you spilled onto each card have been carefully placed in my Bible. I re-read those words when I'm feeling happy or sad. I even think of our back porch conversations and the wisdom you've shared. I'm thankful to have you as my aunt and spiritual teacher. You are so warm and loving. You make this world a better place.

Dani Johnson- Thank you for following God's instruction and helping others become the best people you know they can be. Thank you for praying fearlessly lying on your face at your business conference. It was in this moment God got a hold of my heart setting it on fire for prayer. I wanted to pray like you and I got goosebumps on my arms. I didn't know how to pray but after seeing you I knew I wanted to learn how.

Fr. Glenn O'Connor- I know you're resting in Heaven and I wanted to say thank you. Thank you for showing me the love of Jesus. It was through your example I felt God's love.

Sr. Rita- I never thought I'd want to write again after leaving your class but as it turns out I wrote a whole book. Thank you for inspiring me throughout the years and pushing me when I wanted to quit. I was blessed to have you as my teacher and appreciate that special story you shared with me so long ago, it means more to me than you'll ever know. I hope you're enjoying Heaven and God lets you know how much I appreciate you.

Clare V.- Thank you for staying after school and helping me. I appreciate all the time you spent helping me grow as a student but mostly as a person. You will always have a special place in my heart.

Kelly Tawney- Thank you for your support and creating apparel supporting my mission. I appreciate you and everything you have done for me. You're a beautiful soul!

Tracy Davis - Thank you for being my friend, supporter, and capturing the pictures I envisioned. Your creativity and skill made my dream photoshoot come true. Thank you!

To my village- the ones who've had a hand in raising me, working with me, and encouraging me-thank you!

I love you all!

ABOUT THE AUTHOR

Kelly Franklin is a teacher, health and wellness advisor helping women recover from abusive relationships and regain self-esteem. She has a BS in Education. As a recovering survivor from an abusive marriage, she wants to share her experiences to help others. She continues to grow daily as she walks through a joyful life always relying on Christian guidance.

Photo credit: Tracy Davis

Email: BeautifullyBrokenkf@gmail.com

instagram.com/the_kelly_franklin
facebook.com/kelly.tharpfranklin
tiktok.com/@Coachkf21

To God Be the Glory